D1309243

# LIGHT & SIMPLE COOKING YEAR-ROUND

# ITALIAN

# GRILLING

LIGHT & SIMPLE COOKING YEAR-ROUND

# ITALIAN

# GRILLING

## JEAN GALTON

### PHOTOGRAPHY BY
## ANN STRATTON

BROADWAY BOOKS · NEW YORK

I T A L I A N   G R I L L I N G

Copyright © 1997 by Smallwood and Stewart. All rights reserved. Printed in
Singapore. No part of this book may be reproduced or transmitted in any form
or by any means, electronic or mechanical, including photocopying, recording,
or by any information storage and retrieval system, without written permission from the
publisher. For information, address Broadway Books, a division of Bantam
Doubleday Dell Publishing Group, Inc., 1540 Broadway, New York, NY 10036.

Broadway Books titles may be purchased for business or promotional use or for special sales.
For information, please write to: Special Markets Department, Bantam
Doubleday Dell Publishing Group, Inc., 1540 Broadway, New York, NY 10036.

BROADWAY BOOKS and its logo, a letter B bisected on the diagonal,
are trademarks of Broadway Books, a division of Bantam Doubleday Dell Publishing Group, Inc.

Library of Congress Cataloging-in-Publication Data

Galton, Jean.
Italian grilling: light and simple cooking year-round / Jean Galton.—1st ed.
p. cm.
ISBN 0-553-06170-4 (pbk.)
1. Barbecue cookery. 2. Cookery, Italian. I. Title.
TX840.B3G35  1997  96-54739
641.5'784—dc21  CIP

FIRST EDITION
Produced by Smallwood and Stewart, Inc., New York

Edited by: Deborah Mintcheff
Designed by: Susi Oberhelman
Food Stylist: Rori Spinelli
Prop Stylist: Denise Canter

ISBN  0-553-06170-4

97 98 99 00 01 10 9 8 7 6 5 4 3 2 1

# CONTENTS

# INTRODUCTION

FOR SEVERAL YEARS, I taught basic cooking lessons at an upscale cooking school. The students learned all sorts of complicated sauces and myriad cooking techniques in just five sessions. The most popular class was always the one on grilling: It was fun and easy, and the freshness of the ingredients made the food absolutely wonderful.

Grilling is the most basic and elemental of cooking techniques, part of our primal past. Simple as this style of cooking is, cooking food over a fire or grill has significant advantages. It is fast and extremely versatile. Meat, poultry, and fish become wonderfully crusty and burnished while remaining tender, moist, and juicy. Vegetables and fruits placed over the same fire are elevated to new heights; their natural sugars caramelize, coloring them a rich brown on the outside while leaving them

succulent and meltingly tender on the inside. Add to this the rich, smoky quality that grilled food takes on and you have a cooking technique that enhances the simplest preparation.

Grilling is ideally suited to our modern preference for low-fat meals consisting of more vegetables and leaner cuts of meat and fish because so little fat is needed. And grilling is also wonderfully suited to Italian cuisine, with its unpretentious love of fresh ingredients and straightforward preparations. Consider fresh vine-ripened tomatoes, for example. When grilled, their rich flavor becomes concentrated and their flesh becomes warm and tender. Take those smoky grilled tomatoes and rub them against thick slices of garlic-rubbed country bread, drizzle lightly with your best olive oil, and sprinkle with slivers of aromatic basil — and you have a feast for your eyes as well as your stomach. This is simple food at its best.

# TYPES OF GRILLS

There are many different types of grills, but for the sake of simplicity, I'll concentrate on the two most popular: gas (which have lids) and covered charcoal grills. Both types will give you the control that simple hibachis and less-expensive charcoal grills just can't. All of the recipes in this book were tested on a basic gas grill.

GAS GRILLS are fast and incredibly easy to use. They don't require matches or starters, you can regulate the heat with the turn of a dial, and they maintain a constant temperature with little effort. Look for one with a good-size cooking surface, and don't worry about fancy dials or needles.

I generally grill with the lid down. It keeps in the heat and smoke (smoke adds flavor) and helps keep the temperature constant. The only time I leave the lid up is when I am grilling quickly cooked foods such as shrimp or bread for bruschetta. These need to be watched carefully, since they can burn in a matter of seconds.

To clean the grill, simply preheat for 5 to 10 minutes, then scrape the grate with a wire brush, crumpled piece of foil, spatula, or grill scraper. If the fire is hot enough, anything left on the grate will simply burn off.

IN COVERED CHARCOAL GRILLS, such as kettle grills, the fire is regulated by opening or closing the vents in the lid and beneath the coals. To start the fire, first open all the vents. Briquettes made of hardwood or coal are the most common fuel. For extra flavor, you can also add mesquite or fruit wood chips or chunks, grapevine cuttings, or fresh and dried herbs onto the coals once the fire is hot. My favorite method of lighting the briquettes is with a chimney starter: a metal cylinder with a grate near its base. Simply put newspaper underneath, set the chimney starter on the grill grate, and pour briquettes into the can. The briquettes will catch fire quickly once the newspaper is ignited. When they are all glowing, empty the briquettes onto the grill grate and put the grill rack in place.

To achieve a good charcoal fire, let the briquettes burn down until they are red or gray-white (ashed-over) and glowing. The more briquettes you use and the higher they are stacked, the longer and hotter the fire. For simple grilled bread, vegetables, and most fish, you'll need only a small amount of coals; for thicker cuts of meat and poultry, you'll need a hotter fire — and more coals.

The most accurate way to determine the temperature of your fire is to use an oven thermometer set on the grill grate. Many people recommend testing the temperature by holding your hand over the coals; this is pretty subjective, but, generally, if you can hold your hand about 5 inches above the coals for no more than about two to three seconds, the fire is considered very hot! If the fire is burning too hot, gradually close the vents until the right temperature is reached.

Since grilling is an outdoor activity, the outdoor temperature and wind can affect your cooking. If it's cold or windy, your grill will have to struggle to maintain heat. Take this into account when building your charcoal fire. Make sure you use enough briquettes on cold days, and keep the grill out of the wind as much as possible. Use the lid (this applies to gas grills as well) to hold the heat in.

After cooking, close the vents and close the lid. The fire will go out from lack of oxygen.

Always make sure your grill is at a safe distance from your house, including any roof overhangs, especially when cooking over charcoal. Keep small children away, or put the grill out of their path. Keep a spritzer bottle of water around for flare-ups and, keep water and/or a fire extinguisher handy.

# ACCESSORIES

**BRUSHES**  I use an inexpensive pastry brush for food, but I never use it on the grill itself. To oil the grill rack, use an oiled cotton rag.

**MEAT THERMOMETER**  I'm a big fan of instant-read meat thermometers, especially for larger pieces of meat. They're fast and accurate.

**OVEN MITTS**  Make sure that you have a good thick pair on hand — grilling temperatures are very high.

**SKEWERS**  Use skewers that are thin and have good sharp points. Inexpensive bamboo skewers are fine; soak them in warm water for thirty minutes before using them.

**SPATULAS**  I like to have two long-handled stainless steel spatulas on hand, especially if I'm grilling fish. Never use wooden or rubber ones.

**TONGS**  I couldn't grill without at least one pair of long stainless-steel tongs for turning the food. Use an inexpensive but sturdy pair.

**VEGETABLE GRILL RACK AND FISH BASKET**  These hinged baskets make it easy to turn smaller or more delicate food and they prevent small items from falling into the coals. Always oil a fish basket before using it to prevent the fish from sticking.

Because the flavors of Italian cooking are so straightforward and simple, it is absolutely essential to seek out the best ingredients. If you don't have access to a local farmer's market, try growing your own herbs and vegetables. Locate a store that carries chunks of real Italian Parmigiano-Reggiano, search out an extra-virgin olive oil that suits your palate, and stock up. In exchange, you will be amply rewarded with wonderful, rich flavors and glorious meals.

# APPETIZERS & SOUPS

# SALAD

## CAPRESE

**Here's a grilled version of the classic tomato, basil, and mozzarella salad. Try to buy freshly smoked mozzarella and firm tomatoes. And use a vegetable grill rack so you don't have to rescue the onion slices from the coals.**

*Serves 4*

IN A SMALL NONREACTIVE SAUCEPAN, bring the orange juice to a boil over high heat. Reduce the heat to medium-low and simmer until reduced to 1 tablespoon. Remove from the heat and whisk in 1 tablespoon of the basil oil. Set aside.

Preheat the grill to high and brush with oil.

Brush the tomato and onion slices on both sides with the remaining 1 tablespoon basil oil and sprinkle with the salt and pepper. Grill the tomato and onion slices for 2 to 4 minutes on each side, or just until charred and softened.

Arrange the tomato, onion, and mozzarella slices in rows, overlapping the slices, on a serving platter. Garnish with the basil, drizzle with the orange dressing, and serve.

¼ cup fresh orange juice

2 tablespoons basil oil*

3 large red or yellow tomatoes, or a combination (about 1½ pounds), cut into ½-inch-thick slices

1 medium-size red onion, cut into ½-inch-thick slices

½ teaspoon salt

½ teaspoon freshly ground pepper

8 ounces smoked mozzarella cheese, cut into ¼-inch-thick slices

¼ cup large fresh basil leaves

**\*available at specialty food stores**

12

# POMODORO

*Serves 6*

**This soup is really just fresh summery tomatoes thickened with hearty country bread and lightly scented with wood smoke. You can grill without the smoking chips, but they add depth of flavor. The texture of the finished soup is coarse; if you prefer a smooth-textured soup, just puree the ingredients.**

IN A SMALL BOWL, soak the wood chips in cold water to cover for 30 minutes. Preheat the grill to high and brush with oil.

Drain the wood chips and place on a piece of foil. Bring the foil up and around the chips, leaving the top open. Place the packet of wood chips directly on the briquettes, cover the grill, and let the smoke build up for about 5 minutes.

Grill the bread for about 2 minutes on each side, or until toasted. Cut the bread into large chunks and set aside.

Grill the tomatoes for 2 to 3 minutes on each side, or until lightly charred and nicely marked. In a food processor, puree the tomatoes. Set aside.

In a large nonreactive pot, heat the oil over high heat. Add the garlic and red pepper flakes and cook, stirring, for about 1 minute, or until the garlic is golden. Add the bread, pureed tomatoes, salt, and water, stirring to combine. Bring to a boil and boil, stirring often, for 3 minutes. Reduce the heat to medium-low and cook, stirring frequently, for 20 minutes, or until thickened. Stir in the basil.

To serve, ladle into soup bowls and sprinkle with the Parmesan.

---

1 cup wood smoking chips

Eight ½-inch-thick large slices country bread

12 plum tomatoes, halved & seeded

¼ cup extra-virgin olive oil

3 garlic cloves, minced

⅛ to ¼ teaspoon crushed red pepper flakes

1 teaspoon salt

3 cups cold water

3 tablespoons chopped fresh basil

Freshly grated Parmesan cheese, for serving

# BASIL POLENTA

*Serves 4*

When grilled, polenta becomes deliciously crusty on the outside while remaining creamy and tender on the inside. Here it's topped with garlicky tomatoes—a terrific way to start a summer meal. Since polenta has a tendency to stick to the grill, generously oil both the grill and the polenta wedges, or you'll never pry them off the grill.

IN A MEDIUM-SIZE HEAVY-BOTTOMED saucepan, bring the milk, water, basil, 1 teaspoon of the salt, and ½ teaspoon of the pepper to a boil over high heat. Slowly add the polenta while whisking constantly in one direction. Reduce the heat to medium-low and cook, stirring constantly with a wooden spoon, for 2 to 4 minutes, or until very thick. Pour the polenta onto an ungreased baking sheet and spread into an 8-inch round. Set aside until firm.

Preheat the grill to high and brush with oil.

In a small bowl, combine the tomatoes, garlic, 2 tablespoons of the oil, and the remaining ½ teaspoon each salt and pepper. Set aside.

Cut the polenta into 8 triangles. Brush the triangles with the remaining 1 tablespoon oil. Grill the polenta for 3 minutes, or until browned on the underside. Turn the polenta triangles over and sprinkle with the mozzarella. Cover the grill and cook for 2 to 3 minutes longer, or until the cheese has melted. Transfer to serving plates, top with the tomato mixture, and serve.

---

2½ cups low-fat (2%) or whole milk

1 cup cold water

¼ cup chopped fresh basil

1½ teaspoons salt

1 teaspoon freshly ground pepper

1 cup imported instant polenta (about 6 ounces)

4 plum tomatoes, halved, seeded & cut into ¼-inch dice

1 garlic clove, minced

3 tablespoons extra-virgin olive oil

1 cup grated smoked mozzarella cheese (4 ounces)

# LEMON-TOMATO TOPPED MUSSELS

*Serves 4*

**P**REHEAT THE GRILL TO HIGH.

In a medium-size bowl, combine the tomatoes, onion, parsley, oregano, lemon zest, garlic, salt, and pepper. Add the oil and toss until well mixed. Set aside.

Place the clams and mussels on the grill. Grill for about 3 to 5 minutes, or until they open, removing them to a serving platter or large shallow bowl as they open. (Discard any that don't open.) Spoon the tomato mixture over the clams and mussels and serve.

**Here is a wonderful way to start a summer meal. Buy small clams and mussels and keep them on ice in the fridge until you are ready to grill. Follow this with pasta tossed with olive oil, basil, and cheese, and serve a green salad on the side.**

- 2 large tomatoes, chopped
- 3 tablespoons finely chopped onion
- 3 tablespoons finely chopped fresh flat-leaf parsley
- 1 tablespoon chopped fresh oregano or ½ teaspoon dried
- ¾ teaspoon grated lemon zest
- 1 small garlic clove, minced
- ½ teaspoon salt
- ¼ teaspoon freshly ground pepper
- 2 tablespoons extra-virgin olive oil
- 1 pound littleneck or manila clams, well scrubbed
- 1 pound medium-size mussels, debearded & well scrubbed

# & FENNEL SALAD

*Serves 4*

**Here, squid are featured in a pretty, colorful salad that combines crunchy fennel, Kalamata olives, and roasted red peppers. You can make the salad up to several hours ahead, but serve it at room temperature for the best flavor.**

PREHEAT THE GRILL to high and brush with oil.

Grill the bell pepper, turning occasionally, for about 15 minutes, or until blackened on all sides. Transfer to a paper bag and let steam for 10 minutes. When cool enough to handle, peel, core, seed, and coarsely chop the pepper. Transfer to a large bowl.

Meanwhile, in a medium-size bowl, toss the squid with 1 tablespoon of the oil and sprinkle with the salt. Grill the squid, turning once, for 1 to 2 minutes, or just until opaque. Cut the bodies crosswise into ¼-inch-thick rings. If the tentacles are large, cut in half.

Put the squid into the bowl with the bell pepper, add the remaining ingredients, and toss until well mixed. Cover and refrigerate for about 30 minutes to allow the flavors to blend.

Serve at room temperature.

---

1 red bell pepper

¾ pound cleaned small squid

3 tablespoons extra-virgin olive oil

½ teaspoon salt

1 large fennel bulb, trimmed, halved lengthwise & thinly sliced

½ cup Kalamata olives, pitted & coarsely chopped

2 scallions, thinly sliced

2 tablespoons chopped fresh basil

¼ cup chopped fresh flat-leaf parsley

2 tablespoons fresh lemon juice

½ teaspoon freshly ground pepper

# PANCETTA-STUFFED

*Serves 4*

These stuffed shrimp are showstoppers. Make sure you pack the stuffing tightly and chill the shrimp thoroughly to firm them up, or you'll lose all the stuffing into the coals.

WITH SMALL KITCHEN SCISSORS, split the shrimp shells down the back. Then, with a small knife, make a lengthwise slit, cutting from front to the back, about three quarters of the way through the shrimp. Remove the veins and rinse the shrimp under cold running water. Pat dry, put on a plate and cover. Refrigerate.

In a small skillet, heat 1 tablespoon of the oil over medium-high heat. Add the onions and cook for about 3 minutes, or until softened. Add the pancetta and cook for about 2 minutes longer, or until the pancetta is golden brown. Transfer to a medium-size bowl. Add the breadcrumbs, tomato, egg, oregano, and pepper, tossing to mix well.

Place a heaping tablespoonful of the filling in the opening of each shrimp, lightly pressing down to compress the stuffing. Refrigerate for at least 30 minutes, or up to 1 hour.

Meanwhile, preheat the grill to high and brush with oil.

Drizzle the shrimp with the remaining 1 tablespoon oil. Grill for 2 to 3 minutes on each side, or just until bright pink and firm to the touch. Remove to a serving platter and serve hot.

12 extra-large shrimp (about 1 pound), unpeeled

2 tablespoons extra-virgin olive oil

½ cup finely chopped onions

¼ pound pancetta, finely chopped

1 cup fresh breadcrumbs

1 plum tomato, halved, seeded & finely chopped

1 large egg, lightly beaten

1 tablespoon plus 1 teaspoon chopped fresh oregano

¼ teaspoon freshly ground pepper

# SWEET PEPPER SOUP

**GRILLED**

The first bell pepper soup I ever encountered was in Italy at Cibrèo, a famous Florentine restaurant. Unfortunately, it's expensive, so my friends and I went to its less costly counterpart, an informal trattoria sharing the same kitchen. Their famous yellow pepper soup was so beautiful and flavorful that I've been hooked on pepper soup ever since.

PREHEAT THE GRILL to high and brush with oil.

Place the peppers on the grill, skin side down. Grill, turning occasionally, for 10 to 15 minutes, or until lightly charred on both sides. Let cool, then coarsely chop the unpeeled peppers.

In a large saucepan, heat 2 tablespoons of the oil over medium-high heat. Add the peppers, onion, and garlic and cook, stirring, for 4 to 6 minutes, or until the onion is softened. Stir in the potato, broth, water, 1 teaspoon of the salt, and ½ teaspoon of the pepper and bring to a boil. Reduce the heat to medium-low and simmer for about 15 minutes, or until the potato is very tender.

In a food processor or blender, puree the soup, in batches, until smooth. Return the soup to the saucepan, cover, and keep hot over very low heat.

Sprinkle the shrimp with the remaining ¼ teaspoon each salt and pepper, and drizzle with the remaining 1 teaspoon oil. Grill the shrimp, turning once, for 1 to 2 minutes, or until bright pink and firm to the touch. Ladle the soup into serving bowls, arrange the shrimp in the center of each bowl, and scatter the basil over.

- 3 red bell peppers, halved, cored & seeded
- 2 tablespoons plus 1 teaspoon extra-virgin olive oil
- 1 medium-size onion, chopped
- 3 garlic cloves, minced
- 1 medium-size russet potato, peeled & coarsely chopped
- 2 cups chicken or vegetable broth
- 1 cup cold water
- 1¼ teaspoons salt
- ¾ teaspoon freshly ground pepper
- 12 small shrimp (about 6 ounces), peeled & deveined
- 2 tablespoons julienned fresh basil

# MUSHROOM SOUP

**The heady flavor of this chunky mushroom soup is enhanced by the addition of dried porcini mushrooms. Make sure to use a vegetable grill rack to hold onto all the mushroom pieces.**

*Serves 4*

PREHEAT THE GRILL to high. Place a vegetable grill rack on top and brush with oil. In a small bowl, pour the water over the dried mushrooms. Let sit for 10 minutes, or until softened. Remove the mushrooms, reserving the liquid. Finely chop the mushrooms and set aside. Strain the mushroom liquid through a paper towel-lined strainer into a small bowl. Set aside.

Grill the fresh mushrooms, turning occasionally, for 3 to 5 minutes, or until browned and tender. Transfer to a medium-size bowl and set aside.

In a large pot, heat 1 tablespoon of the oil over high heat. Add the onion and garlic and cook, stirring frequently, for 3 to 4 minutes, or until the onion is softened. Add the fresh and dried mushrooms, tomato paste, thyme, broth, reserved mushroom liquid, salt, and pepper, stirring to blend in the tomato paste. Bring to a boil, reduce the heat to medium-low, and simmer for 10 minutes.

Ladle the soup into soup bowls, drizzle with the remaining 1 tablespoon oil, and sprinkle with the Parmesan.

1 cup boiling water

½ ounce dried porcini mushrooms (about ½ cup)

1 pound cremini mushrooms or a combination such as shiitake & button, cut into ½-inch pieces

2 tablespoons extra-virgin olive oil

1 medium-size onion, chopped

2 garlic cloves, minced

1 tablespoon tomato paste

2 large sprigs fresh thyme

2 cups vegetable or chicken broth

½ teaspoon salt

½ teaspoon freshly ground pepper

¼ cup freshly grated Parmesan cheese

# CHICKEN UNDER A BRICK

*Serves 4*

PLACE THE CHICKEN BREAST side down on a cutting board. With kitchen scissors or a large sharp knife, split the chicken along one side of the backbone. Place the chicken skin side up and flatten it by pressing down with the heel of your hand. Drizzle with the oil and sprinkle with the red pepper flakes. Put into a large bowl and distribute half the lemon and all the garlic evenly over the chicken. Cover and marinate in the refrigerator for at least 2 hours, or overnight, turning occasionally.

Preheat the grill to medium-low and brush with oil. Wrap 2 clean bricks in foil.

Discard the lemon and garlic from the chicken. Sprinkle the chicken with the salt. Place the chicken flat on the grill, skin side up, and place the bricks on top. Cover the grill and grill for 15 minutes, or until deep golden, checking to make sure it isn't burning. Turn the chicken over and grill for 15 minutes longer, or until an instant read thermometer inserted into the thigh registers 170°F (or the juices run clear when the thigh is pierced with a small knife. Remove the bricks. Transfer the chicken to a cutting board. Cover the chicken loosely and let rest for 10 minutes.

Meanwhile, grill the remaining lemon slices for 2 to 4 minutes on each side, or grill marked. Cut the chicken into quarters. Put on a serving platter, garnish with the grilled lemon slices, and serve.

A popular dish found in most trattorias throughout Italy, Chicken Under a Brick (or Pollo al Mattone) is a truly inspired way of preparing chicken. Weighted down during cooking, the chicken becomes succulent and flavorful with crispy brown skin. If you don't have any bricks, use a heavy pot filled with water. Serve the chicken with a green salad and crusty bread.

One 3-pound chicken
¼ cup extra-virgin olive oil
1 teaspoon crushed red pepper flakes

2 lemons, washed & sliced
6 large garlic cloves, smashed
1 teaspoon salt

# AGLIATA

## CHICKEN

Here's a recipe for garlic addicts–the stuffing contains generous amounts of both roasted and raw garlic. (By the way, when you serve this dish, don't add garlic to any of the side dishes— you'll get your fill here.)

*Serves 4*

PREHEAT THE OVEN to 400°F.

Wrap the head of garlic in foil and roast for about 1 hour, or until very soft. When cool, squeeze the garlic pulp from each clove. Mash the garlic and set aside.

Preheat the grill to low and brush with oil.

Put the breadcrumbs, water, and lemon juice in a bowl. Set aside for 5 minutes.

Knead the breadcrumb mixture into a thick paste, adding additional water if needed. Add 1 tablespoon of the oil, the parsley, the mashed and minced garlic, ½ teaspoon of the salt and ½ teaspoon of the pepper, blending well.

Gently slip your fingers under the skin of the chicken breasts and legs to separate the skin from the meat. Spread the stuffing evenly over the breast and leg meat, replace the skin, and secure the skin with toothpicks if necessary. Brush with the remaining 1 tablespoon oil, and sprinkle with the remaining ½ teaspoon salt and 1/4 teaspoon pepper.

Place the chicken on the outer edge of the grill, where it is coolest. Grill for about 20 minutes on each side, or until an instant read thermometer registers 170°F (or the juices run clean when the chicken is pierced between the thigh and breast with a small knife). Cover and let rest for 10 minutes. Serve hot or at room temperature.

1 head garlic, papery skin removed & top 1 inch cut off, plus 1 large garlic clove, minced

1 cup fresh breadcrumbs

¼ cup cold water

1 tablespoon fresh lemon juice

2 tablespoons extra-virgin olive oil

1 tablespoon chopped fresh flat-leaf parsley

1 teaspoon salt

¾ teaspoon freshly ground pepper

One 3-pound chicken, split in half

# LEMON-OREGANO

*Serves 4*

COMBINE THE FRESH OREGANO, dried oregano, salt, pepper, lemon juice, and oil in a small dish. Using your fingers, spread the herb mixture over both sides of the chicken. Put the chicken on a plate, cover with plastic wrap, and marinate in the refrigerator for 1 hour.

Preheat the grill to high and brush with oil.

Grill the chicken for 3 to 5 minutes on each side, or until just cooked through. Transfer to a small platter and serve hot.

Don't be alarmed by the amount of oregano in this recipe. Dried and fresh oregano have very different flavors and are balanced here by the addition of fresh lemon juice. Penne tossed with chopped fresh tomatoes, and a green salad, will make this a quick and satisfying meal.

¼ cup chopped fresh oregano

1 tablespoon dried oregano, crumbled

½ teaspoon salt

½ teaspoon freshly ground pepper

2 tablespoons fresh lemon juice

1 tablespoon extra-virgin olive oil

4 boneless skinless chicken breast halves (about 5 ounces each)

# CHICKEN

## DEVILED

**Pollo alla Diavola, a traditional Italian dish, is a simple way of preparing chicken. Marinating chicken breasts in olive oil with red pepper flakes and black pepper creates a fiery bird, its heat somewhat doused by the addition of fresh lemon.**

*Serves 4*

IN A MEDIUM-SIZE BOWL, sprinkle the chicken with the oil, pepper, and red pepper flakes. Add the garlic, cover the bowl with plastic wrap, and marinate in the refrigerator for 4 to 6 hours.

Preheat the grill to high and brush with oil.

Sprinkle the chicken with the salt. Grill for 3 to 5 minutes on each side, or until just cooked through. Transfer to a serving platter and garnish with the lemon slices. Serve hot or at room temperature.

---

4 boneless skinless chicken breast halves (about 5 ounces each)

2 tablespoons extra-virgin olive oil

1 teaspoon coarsely ground pepper, or more to taste

½ teaspoon crushed red pepper flakes

3 garlic cloves, smashed

½ teaspoon salt

1 lemon, thickly sliced, for garnish

# SAGE-STUFFED CHICKEN

*Serves 4*

The short ingredient list for this recipe belies its tastiness. Make sure the Fontina cheese you purchase is Italian, not Danish Fontina—the taste and texture are totally different.

PREHEAT THE GRILL to high and brush with oil.

Place a chicken breast on a work surface. Using a thin sharp knife, slice the chicken horizontally in half, using a slight back-and-forth motion. Place the chicken between 2 pieces of plastic wrap and lightly pound to ⅛-inch thickness, taking care not to tear the chicken. Repeat with the remaining chicken.

Place a slice of prosciutto, a slice of Fontina, and a sage leaf on each piece of chicken. Beginning with the narrow end, roll up the chicken and secure with toothpicks. Brush the rolls with the oil and sprinkle with the salt and pepper.

Grill the chicken rolls, turning occasionally, for 7 to 8 minutes, or until browned on all sides and cooked through. Transfer to a serving platter, remove the toothpicks, and serve.

4 boneless skinless chicken breast halves (about 5 ounces each)

8 thin slices prosciutto

8 thin slices Italian Fontina cheese

8 fresh sage leaves

1 tablespoon extra-virgin olive oil

½ teaspoon salt

½ teaspoon freshly ground pepper

# ROSEMARY-SCENTED CHICKEN

The combination of rosemary and fine balsamic vinegar makes this a very special dish. Buy the best quality balsamic vinegar your budget will allow, and be sure to use fresh rosemary. Dried rosemary simply isn't right for this recipe.

PREHEAT THE GRILL to high and brush with oil.

In a mortar and pestle, combine the rosemary, garlic, salt, and pepper. Mash until pureed, then stir in the oil. (Alternatively, using a large knife, very finely chop the garlic and rosemary with the salt. Put into a small bowl and stir in the pepper and oil.) Spread evenly over both sides of the chicken.

Grill the chicken for 3 to 5 minutes on each side, or until just cooked through. Transfer to a serving platter and drizzle with the balsamic vinegar. Serve hot or at room temperature.

¼ cup chopped fresh rosemary

2 large garlic cloves

1 teaspoon salt

1 teaspoon freshly ground pepper

2 tablespoons extra-virgin olive oil

4 boneless skinless chicken breast halves (about 5 ounces each)

2 tablespoons very good quality balsamic vinegar

**TIP:** To make your grilled chicken breasts look like restaurant fare, place them on the grill for about 2 minutes. Then give them a quarter turn and continue cooking for 1 or 2 minutes longer. Turn the chicken over and repeat the procedure. You will end up with very professional looking crosshatch-marked chicken.

# FENNEL-ANISE CHICKEN

**Surprisingly, fennel grow wild everywhere around Seattle, a place quite unlike fennel's native homeland on the shores of the Mediterranean. I love its subtle licorice-like flavor. Here, it's combined with anise, which has a very similar flavor, but is a bit sweeter and a little more intense.**

IN A SMALL SKILLET, toast the fennel and anise seeds over high heat for 1 to 2 minutes, or until lightly browned. Transfer the seeds to a food processor and process until finely chopped. Add the garlic and process until pureed. Add the wine, oil, and pepper, and pulse until blended.

Put the chicken into a medium-size bowl and spread the marinade evenly all over the chicken. Cover with plastic wrap, and marinate in the refrigerator for at least 2 hours, or overnight.

Preheat the grill to high and brush with oil.

Sprinkle the chicken with the salt. Grill the chicken for 3 to 5 minutes on each side, or just until cooked through. Sprinkle with the parsley and serve.

2 teaspoons fennel seeds

1 teaspoon anise seeds

2 garlic cloves

2 tablespoons dry white wine

1 tablespoon extra-virgin olive oil

½ teaspoon freshly ground pepper

1½ pounds boneless skinless chicken thighs

½ teaspoon salt

1 tablespoon chopped fresh flat-leaf parsley

*Serves 4*

These grilled Cornish hens are served with a sauce for real anchovy lovers. The sauce is also delicious on grilled bread and on grilled fish such as halibut or swordfish.

PREHEAT THE GRILL to medium-low and brush with oil.

Brush the Cornish hens with 1 tablespoon of the oil, then sprinkle with the salt and pepper.

Grill the hens for about 15 minutes on each side, or until cooked through (the juices should run clear when the hen is pierced with a small knife between the thigh and breast). Remove to a platter, cover, and let rest for 10 minutes.

Meanwhile, in a small serving dish, combine the anchovies, parsley, capers, thyme, garlic, and the remaining 3 tablespoons oil. Let stand for at least 10 minutes.

Just before serving, briefly whisk the anchovy sauce. Serve alongside the hens.

**4 Cornish hens (about 1½ pounds each), split in half**

**¼ cup extra-virgin olive oil**

**½ teaspoon salt**

**½ teaspoon freshly ground pepper**

**6 anchovy fillets, minced**

**2 tablespoons chopped fresh flat-leaf parsley**

**2 tablespoons capers, rinsed**

**1 tablespoon fresh thyme leaves**

**1 garlic clove, minced**

# CORNISH HENS

SAVORY

**Cornish hens grill beautifully when stuffed under the skin with this aromatic stuffing. Today, there are lots of wonderful artisanal bakers, and their breads make exquisite breadcrumbs. If possible, make the stuffing with olive bread—it adds one more layer of flavor.**

*Serves 4 to 6*

PREHEAT THE GRILL to medium-low and brush with oil.

In a medium-size skillet, heat 1 tablespoon of the oil over medium-high heat. Add the onions and garlic and cook for 3 to 4 minutes, or until the onions are softened. Transfer to a medium-size bowl and add the breadcrumbs, prosciutto, egg, Parmesan, parsley, sage, ¼ teaspoon of the salt, and ¼ teaspoon of the pepper, stirring until mixed well.

Gently slip your fingers under the skin of the breast and leg meat of the hens to separate the skin from the meat without removing it entirely, and taking care not to tear the skin. Carefully spread the stuffing evenly over the breast and leg meat. Secure the skin with toothpicks if necessary. Brush the hens with the remaining 1 tablespoon oil and sprinkle with the remaining ½ teaspoon each salt and pepper.

Grill the hens for 15 to 17 minutes on each side, or until cooked through (the juices should run clear when the hen is pierced with a small knife between the thigh and breast). Cover and let rest for 10 minutes before serving.

2 tablespoons extra-virgin olive oil

¾ cup chopped onions

1 garlic clove, minced

1 cup fresh breadcrumbs

2 slices prosciutto, finely chopped

1 large egg, lightly beaten

2 tablespoons freshly grated Parmesan cheese

2 tablespoons chopped fresh flat-leaf parsley

1 tablespoon chopped fresh sage or 1 teaspoon dried

¾ teaspoon salt

¾ teaspoon freshly ground pepper

4 Cornish hens (about 1½ pounds each), split in half

# PORK WITH ORANGE

*Serves 4*

This pretty pork dish needs to marinate overnight to allow the meat to absorb the marinade flavors. If you're usually scared off by anchovies, don't be. These little fish add depth of flavor, but are otherwise quite undetectable.

IN A SHALLOW BAKING DISH, combine the anchovies, garlic, fennel, honey, and oil. Add the pork cubes and orange slices, tossing to coat evenly. Cover and marinate overnight in the refrigerator.

Preheat the grill to medium-high and brush with oil.

Thread the pork and orange slices alternately onto 6 metal skewers and season with the salt and pepper.

Grill for 5 to 6 minutes on each side, or until the pork is cooked through but not dry. Transfer the skewers to a platter and serve.

4 anchovy fillets, finely chopped

4 garlic cloves, smashed

1 tablespoon fennel seeds, crushed

2 tablespoons honey

2 tablespoons extra-virgin olive oil

1½ pounds pork loin, trimmed & cut into 1½-inch cubes

2 small navel oranges, washed & cut into ¼-inch-thick slices

1 teaspoon salt

½ teaspoon freshly ground pepper

# MARINATED PORK

*Serves 4*

**Here's a recipe for thinly sliced pork chops that marinate in a mixture of orange zest, lemon zest, and mixed herbs. American pork is bred to be very lean, so be sure not to overcook the chops, or they'll be dry.**

IN A LARGE SHALLOW DISH, combine the parsley, rosemary, oregano, orange zest, lemon zest, garlic, sugar, pepper, and oil, mixing until blended. Using your fingers, spread the herb mixture evenly over the pork. Cover and marinate in the refrigerator for at least 8 hours, or overnight.

Preheat the grill to high and brush with oil.

Scrape the marinade off the pork chops and sprinkle them with the salt. Grill the pork chops for 2 to 3 minutes on each side for medium, or to the desired degree of doneness. Serve hot.

¼ cup packed fresh flat-leaf parsley, coarsely chopped

1 tablespoon chopped fresh rosemary

½ teaspoon dried oregano

1 tablespoon grated orange zest

1 tablespoon grated lemon zest

2 garlic cloves, chopped

1 teaspoon sugar

½ teaspoon freshly ground pepper

2 tablespoons extra-virgin olive oil

Six ½-inch-thick rib pork chops

½ teaspoon salt

# PORK WITH AUTUMN

*Serves 4*

TOAST THE FENNEL SEEDS in a small skillet over medium heat for 2 to 3 minutes, or until fragrant. Transfer the fennel seeds to a spice grinder or mortar and pestle and add the juniper berries. Pulse or grind until crushed.

In a large shallow dish, combine the fennel-juniper mixture, thyme, bay leaves, garlic, sugar, pepper, and oil, stirring until mixed. Using your fingers, spread the mixture evenly over the pork. Cover and marinate in the refrigerator for at least 8 hours, or overnight.

Preheat the grill to high and brush with oil.

Scrape the marinade off the pork and sprinkle the meat with the salt. Grill the pork, turning several times, for about 10 minutes, or until an instant read thermometer registers about 155°F when inserted in the center of the pork. Transfer to a cutting board, cover loosely with foil, and let stand for 5 minutes before cutting into ¼-inch-thick slices. Transfer to a platter and serve.

**Pork tenderloin is one of the most flavorful of the leaner cuts of meat. Serve this pork loin with a celery, toasted walnut, and bitter greens salad and a rice pilaf.**

1 tablespoon fennel seeds

1 tablespoon juniper berries

8 large sprigs fresh thyme

2 imported bay leaves, broken in half

3 garlic cloves, mashed to a paste

1 tablespoon sugar

½ teaspoon freshly ground pepper

2 tablespoons extra-virgin olive oil

1½ pounds pork tenderloin, trimmed

½ teaspoon salt

# VEAL WITH ARUGULA SALAD

*Serves 4*

My favorite way to eat often involves one dish with plenty of salad. This classic Roman dish of grilled veal chops with a sprightly arugula salad definitely fits that category. Make this at the end of the summer, when tomatoes and arugula are at their peak.

IN A LARGE SHALLOW BAKING DISH, combine 2 tablespoons of the oil, 2 tablespoons of the balsamic vinegar, the mustard, and garlic. Add the veal chops, turning to coat well. Cover and marinate in the refrigerator for 1 to 3 hours.

Preheat the grill to medium and brush with oil.

Sprinkle the veal chops with ½ teaspoon of the salt and ½ teaspoon of the pepper. Grill the chops for 4 to 5 minutes on each side, or until just cooked through. Transfer to serving plates and cover loosely to keep warm.

Put the arugula, tomatoes, and onion in a large bowl. In a small jar with a tight-fitting lid, combine the remaining 2 tablespoons oil, the remaining 1 tablespoon balsamic vinegar, and the remaining ¼ teaspoon each salt and pepper. Cover the jar and shake well. Pour the dressing over the arugula salad and toss until well coated. Place the arugula salad over the veal chops and serve immediately.

¼ cup extra-virgin olive oil

3 tablespoons balsamic vinegar

2 tablespoons grainy mustard

2 large garlic cloves, minced

Four ½-inch-thick veal chops (8 to 10 ounces each), lightly flattened with the palm of your hand

¾ teaspoon salt

¾ teaspoon freshly ground pepper

2 bunches arugula, trimmed & washed

2 medium-size tomatoes, chopped

⅓ cup chopped red onion

# TOMATO BRUSCHETTA

**SPIEDINI WITH**

**Here are luscious grilled meatballs, perfumed with bay leaves and accompanied by a very simple tomato bruschetta. Make sure you buy imported Turkish bay leaves, not California bay laurel—there's a huge difference in the taste.**

SOAK FOUR 8-INCH BAMBOO SKEWERS in cold water for at least 30 minutes. Put the bay leaves into a small bowl, add boiling water to cover, and soak for 30 minutes; drain well.

Preheat the grill to high and brush with oil.

In a large bowl, combine the pork, veal, beef, breadcrumbs, Parmesan, egg, parsley, basil, oregano, and ½ teaspoon each salt and pepper. Stir with a fork until well blended. Using wet hands, roll the mixture into 16 meatballs. Thread the meatballs and softened bay leaves alternately onto the skewers.

Grill the spiedini, turning occasionally, for 8 to 10 minutes, or until browned on all sides. Remove to a platter and cover loosely to keep warm.

Meanwhile, brush the bread with the oil. Grill for about 2 minutes on each side, or until golden brown. Rub the garlic over one side of the bread slices. Rub the cut side of the tomatoes into the bread, pressing them so all the tomato juices and flesh are rubbed into the bread; discard the skin. Sprinkle with ½ teaspoon salt and serve alongside the spiedini.

12 imported bay leaves

½ pound ground pork

¼ pound each ground veal & lean ground beef

½ cup each dried bread-crumbs & freshly grated Parmesan cheese

1 large egg, lightly beaten

2 tablespoons each chopped fresh flat-leaf parsley & basil

1 teaspoon dried oregano, crumbled

Salt & freshly ground pepper

Eight ½-inch-thick slices crusty country bread

2 tablespoons extra-virgin olive oil

2 garlic cloves, halved

2 large tomatoes, halved & seeded

# LAMB CHOPS

*Serves 4*

**This Roman dish literally means "burning fingers." It's a wonderful treatment of thin-cut rib lamb chops. Brown and crisp on the outside, tender and rare on the inside, these chops are meant to be picked up and eaten with your fingers.**

COMBINE THE OIL AND red pepper flakes in a small dish. Put the lamb into a shallow nonreactive dish. Brush or use your fingers to rub the peppered oil all over the chops. Place the lemon slices and rosemary sprigs on top. Cover with plastic wrap and marinate in the refrigerator for at least 3 hours, or overnight.

Preheat the grill to high and brush with oil.

Discard the lemon slices and rosemary sprigs. Sprinkle the lamb with the salt. Grill the lamb for 2 to 3 minutes on each side for medium-rare, or to the desired degree of doneness. Transfer to a platter and serve.

3 tablespoons extra-virgin olive oil

¼ teaspoon crushed red pepper flakes

Eight ½-inch-thick rib lamb chops

1 lemon, thinly sliced

6 large sprigs fresh rosemary

1 teaspoon salt

# TUSCAN WHITE BEANS

**DUCK WITH**

Walk into any restaurant in Tuscany and you will most likely find white beans on the menu. In fact, many Italians refer to Tuscans as mangiafagioli or "bean eaters" (not necessarily a compliment). I find these slowly cooked white beans scented with garlic, sage, and olive oil irresistible.

IN A LARGE BOWL, soak the beans overnight in cold water to cover by 3 inches. Meanwhile, marinate the duck: Combine the rosemary, parsley, white wine, and 2 tablespoons of the oil in a medium-size bowl. Add the duck, turning to coat. Cover with plastic wrap and marinate in the refrigerator for at least 3 hours, or overnight.

Drain the beans, rinse under cold water, and drain again. Put the beans, sage, and garlic in a medium-size saucepan and add water to cover by 3 inches. Bring to a simmer over medium heat and cook for 30 minutes. Add ½ teaspoon salt and continue cooking for 10 to 20 minutes longer, or until the beans are very tender. Drain the beans, discarding the sage, and return to the saucepan. Add the remaining 2 tablespoons oil, ¼ teaspoon salt and ½ teaspoon pepper. Toss to mix and cover to keep warm. Preheat the grill to medium-hot and brush with oil.

Remove the duck and sprinkle with ½ teaspoon each salt and pepper. Grill for 3 to 4 minutes on each side for medium-rare. Transfer to a cutting board, cover, and let rest for 5 minutes.

Using a sharp knife, thinly slice the duck against the grain. Place some beans on each serving plate, arrange the sliced duck on top, and garnish with the sage leaves, if using.

---

½ pound dried Great Northern beans

3 fresh rosemary sprigs, broken up

3 tablespoons chopped fresh flat-leaf parsley

2 tablespoons dry white wine

¼ cup olive oil

2 whole boneless skinless duck breasts, split

12 large fresh sage leaves

4 large garlic cloves

Salt & freshly ground pepper

Fresh sage leaves, for garnish (optional)

# RED WINE-MARINATED RABBIT

Serves 4

Rabbit makes great eating, although most Americans can be a bit tentative about consuming it. Here, the rabbit is marinated for two days, which adds moisture and fragrant herbal overtones. Rabbit is available fresh in most butcher shops and frozen in some grocery stores.

IN A LARGE SHALLOW NONREACTIVE DISH or heavy duty plastic bag, combine the sage, rosemary, bay leaves, garlic, pepper, wine, oil, and vinegar, mixing well. Add the rabbit, turning to coat evenly. Cover and marinate in the refrigerator for 2 days, turning the rabbit several times.

Preheat the grill to medium-low and brush with oil.

Remove the rabbit from the marinade, reserving the marinade. Sprinkle the rabbit on both sides with the salt.

Grill the rabbit for about 15 minutes on each side, or until cooked through; an instant read meat thermometer should register 145°F. Remove to a platter and cover to keep warm.

Meanwhile, pour the marinade into a small nonreactive saucepan and bring to a boil over high heat. Reduce the heat to medium and simmer for about 10 minutes, or until reduced to ½ cup. Strain the marinade and return to the saucepan over low heat. Add the butter, a few pieces at a time, whisking just until incorporated. Transfer to a sauceboat and serve alongside the rabbit.

10 fresh sage leaves

8 large sprigs fresh rosemary

3 imported bay leaves

6 garlic cloves, smashed

½ teaspoon freshly ground pepper

1 cup dry red wine

⅓ cup extra-virgin olive oil

3 tablespoons balsamic vinegar

One 3½-pound rabbit, cut into 6 pieces

1½ teaspoons salt

2 tablespoons unsalted butter, cut into small pieces

*Serves 4*

IN A SMALL BOWL, stir together the parsley, basil, rosemary, garlic, and oil. Spread the herb mixture in the cavity of the fish, dividing it evenly. Put the fish on a plate, cover with plastic wrap, and refrigerate until ready to grill or up to 2 hours.

Preheat the grill to medium-high and brush with oil.

Sprinkle the fish with the salt and pepper. Grill the fish for 4 to 5 minutes on each side, or until cooked through. (It will take about 10 minutes for each inch of thickness.) With 2 spatulas, transfer the fish to a serving platter. Garnish with the lemon wedges and serve.

2 tablespoons finely chopped fresh flat-leaf parsley

2 tablespoons chopped fresh basil

1 tablespoon finely chopped fresh rosemary

2 garlic cloves, finely chopped

2 tablespoons extra-virgin olive oil

2 rainbow or brook trout (about 1 pound each), cleaned, but with heads & tails left on

½ teaspoon salt

½ teaspoon freshly ground pepper

Lemon wedges, for garnish

# SWORDFISH WITH

*Serves 4*

In Italy, swordfish is known as *pesce spada*. It's very commonly grilled, especially in the south. Cook the fish no more than eight minutes per inch of thickness, or it will be overcooked and dry.

WITH A SHARP KNIFE, peel the oranges, making sure to remove all the white pith. Holding an orange over a medium-size bowl, remove the orange sections by cutting with a small knife along the membranes, letting the sections and juice fall into the bowl. Repeat with the remaining oranges. Add the olives, mint, onion, red pepper flakes, 1 tablespoon of the oil, and the lemon juice to the orange sections, gently stirring to combine. Set aside in the refrigerator.

Preheat the grill to high and brush with oil.

Brush the swordfish with the remaining 1 tablespoon oil and sprinkle with the salt and pepper. Grill for 2 to 3 minutes on each side, just until cooked through. Transfer to serving plates, top with the orange salad, and serve.

**3 large navel oranges**

**8 oil-cured black olives, pitted & coarsely chopped**

**2 tablespoons chopped fresh mint**

**2 tablespoons finely chopped red onion**

**Pinch of crushed red pepper flakes**

**2 tablespoons extra-virgin olive oil**

**2 teaspoons fresh lemon juice**

**Four $\frac{1}{2}$-inch-thick swordfish steaks (about 6 ounces each)**

**$\frac{1}{2}$ teaspoon salt**

**$\frac{1}{2}$ teaspoon freshly ground pepper**

# ROMANO

## SWORDFISH

It's a little tricky to pound the swordfish for these rolls, but well worth the effort. The fish stays moist and tender, and the stuffing resounds with southern Italian flavors. If your swordfish is sold in precut half-inch-thick steaks, slice them in half horizontally to make quarter-inch-thick steaks.

PREHEAT THE GRILL TO HIGH and brush generously with oil.

Place each swordfish steak between 2 pieces of plastic wrap. With a meat pounder or the bottom of a pot, pound to a ⅛-inch thickness, being careful not to tear the fish. Cut each piece of fish into 2 rectangles. Put on a plate, cover with plastic wrap, and refrigerate.

In a medium-size skillet, heat 1 tablespoon of the oil over high heat. Add the scallions and garlic and cook, stirring, for 2 to 3 minutes, or until softened. Transfer to a medium-size bowl and add the breadcrumbs, tomatoes, egg, Romano, parsley, mint, and ¼ teaspoon of the pepper, stirring until well mixed.

Put a piece of swordfish on a work surface, with a long side facing you. Place a heaping tablespoon of the stuffing along the bottom edge and roll up jelly-roll style. Secure with 1 or 2 toothpicks. Stuff and roll the remaining fish. Brush the swordfish rolls with the remaining 2 tablespoons oil and sprinkle with the salt and the remaining ¼ teaspoon pepper.

Grill the swordfish rolls, turning to brown on all sides, for 4 to 5 minutes, or until cooked through. Transfer to a platter and serve.

Four ¼-inch-thick swordfish steaks (about 4 ounces each)

3 tablespoons extra-virgin olive oil

⅓ cup chopped scallions

1 garlic clove, minced

1 cup fresh breadcrumbs

2 plum tomatoes, halved, seeded & finely chopped

1 large egg, lightly beaten

2 tablespoons freshly grated Pecorino Romano cheese

2 tablespoons chopped fresh flat-leaf parsley

1 tablespoon chopped fresh mint

½ teaspoon freshly ground pepper

½ teaspoon salt

# FENNEL-RUBBED FISH

*Serves 4*

**It's really worth the extra effort to toast the fennel seeds for this recipe. The seeds become very fragrant and crisp—a delicious coating for the fish.**

TOAST THE FENNEL SEEDS in a small skillet over high heat for 1 to 2 minutes, or until fragrant. Transfer to a mortar and pestle or spice grinder and finely crush. In a small dish, combine the crushed fennel, ½ teaspoon of the salt, and ½ teaspoon of the pepper, mixing well. Brush the halibut on both sides with 1 tablespoon of the oil and sprinkle with the fennel mixture. Put on a plate, cover, and refrigerate for 1 to 3 hours.

Preheat the grill to high and brush with oil.

In a large bowl, drizzle the sliced fennel with the remaining 2 tablespoons oil, tossing until evenly coated. Sprinkle the fennel and tomatoes with the remaining ½ teaspoon each salt and pepper. Set aside.

Grill the halibut for 3 to 4 minutes on each side, or just until cooked through. Transfer to a large platter, cover, and set aside. Grill the tomatoes and fennel for 1 to 3 minutes on each side, or until tender. Remove to the platter.

Place a halibut steak on each serving plate, and top with the tomato and fennel slices. Sprinkle with the chopped fennel and serve.

1 tablespoon fennel seeds

1 teaspoon salt

1 teaspoon freshly ground pepper

Four ½-inch-thick halibut steaks (about 6 ounces each)

3 tablespoons extra-virgin olive oil

2 fennel bulbs, trimmed & cut lengthwise into ¼-inch-thick slices, feathery tops chopped, for garnish

2 large firm tomatoes (about 1 pound), cut into ½-inch-thick slices

# GREMOLATA

**Gremolata is a flavorful mix of lemon zest, chopped garlic, and parsley. Traditionally, it is served with osso buco (braised veal shanks). Here, it's mixed with toasted breadcrumbs and sprinkled on grilled salmon.**

*Serves 6*

IN A MEDIUM-SIZE SKILLET, heat 2 tablespoons of the oil over medium-high heat. Add the breadcrumbs and saute for about 5 minutes, or until the breadcrumbs are toasted. Transfer to a small bowl and stir in the parsley, garlic, lemon zest, orange zest, $\frac{1}{2}$ teaspoon of the salt, and $\frac{1}{2}$ teaspoon of the pepper. Set aside.

Preheat the grill to high and brush with oil.

Brush the salmon with the remaining 1 tablespoon oil and sprinkle with the remaining $\frac{1}{2}$ teaspoon each salt and pepper. Place the salmon skin side down on the grill. Grill for 4 to 5 minutes on each side, or until just cooked through. Transfer to serving plates, sprinkle with the gremolata, and serve.

3 tablespoons extra-virgin olive oil

1½ cups fresh breadcrumbs (made from country bread)

3 tablespoons chopped fresh flat-leaf parsley

1 large garlic clove, minced

1 teaspoon grated lemon zest

1 teaspoon grated orange zest

1 teaspoon salt

1 teaspoon freshly ground pepper

6 salmon fillets (about 6 ounces each), skin left on

# BASIL MAYONNAISE

**SHRIMP WITH**

When you grill unpeeled shrimp, you get to nibble on the shells, getting the seasonings all over your fingers. Then as you peel them, the seasonings transfer back onto the shrimp. The salmonella cloud lurking over homemade mayonnaise is somewhat threatening so I recommend using a good-quality commercial mayonnaise instead.

PREHEAT THE GRILL to high and brush with oil.

Using small kitchen scissors, make a lengthwise slit down the back of each shrimp, cutting partway through the meat. Remove the veins and rinse the shrimp under cold running water. Pat dry with paper towels and put into a medium-size bowl. Drizzle with the oil, tossing to coat evenly, then sprinkle with the salt and ½ teaspoon of the pepper.

In a small bowl, combine the mayonnaise, basil, scallions, anchovies, lemon zest, and the remaining ¼ teaspoon pepper. Transfer to a small serving dish and set aside.

Grill the shrimp for about 2 minutes on each side, or until bright pink and firm to the touch. Transfer to a serving platter and serve accompanied by the basil mayonnaise.

16 jumbo shrimp (about 1½ pounds), unpeeled

1 tablespoon extra-virgin olive oil

½ teaspoon salt

¾ teaspoon freshly ground pepper

1 cup mayonnaise or light mayonnaise

1 cup packed fresh basil leaves

4 scallions, cut into 1-inch lengths

2 anchovy fillets, coarsely chopped

2 teaspoons grated lemon zest

*Serves 4*

SHRIMP

Jumbo shrimp are spectacular when grilled. Since it's nearly impossible to get fresh shrimp (they're almost always frozen as soon as they're caught), ask your fishmonger for a sniff before you buy them. Shrimp should smell like the ocean and not a bit fishy.

PREPARE THE GRILL to high and brush with oil.

Place a sage leaf and a little of the lemon zest on one piece of prosciutto and wrap the prosciutto around a shrimp. Thread an 8- to 10-inch metal skewer through the tail and body of the shrimp. Repeat with the remaining shrimp, threading 4 shrimp onto each skewer. Brush the wrapped shrimp with 1 tablespoon of the oil and sprinkle with the pepper.

Grill the shrimp for about 2 minutes on each side, or until bright pink and firm to the touch. Transfer to a platter, drizzle with the remaining 1 tablespoon oil, and garnish with the lemon wedges. Serve hot.

16 large fresh sage leaves

1 tablespoon grated lemon zest

8 thin slices prosciutto, cut crosswise in half

16 jumbo shrimp (about 1½ pounds), peeled & deveined

2 tablespoons extra-virgin olive oil

½ teaspoon freshly ground pepper

Lemon wedges, for garnish

# LINGUINE WITH SHRIMP

**This recipe commits an Italian heresy, combining seafood and cheese. But times have changed, cooking rules have loosened up, and it tastes great.**

*Serves 4*

SOAK EIGHT 8- to 10-inch bamboo skewers in cold water for 30 minutes.

Thread the shrimp and tomatoes alternately onto the skewers, putting 3 or 4 shrimp and 2 or 3 cherry tomatoes onto each skewer. Brush with 1 tablespoon of the oil, and sprinkle with ½ teaspoon of the salt and ½ teaspoon of the pepper. Put on a plate, cover, and refrigerate until ready to grill.

Preheat the grill to high and brush with oil.

Bring a large pot of water to a rolling boil and add salt to taste. Cook the linguine according to the package directions until al dente. While the pasta is cooking, grill the shrimp for 2 minutes on each side, or until bright pink and firm to the touch.

Reserve ¼ cup of the pasta water. Drain the pasta, then transfer to a large serving bowl. Add the reserved pasta water, the remaining ¼ cup oil, the parsley, basil, mint, rosemary, the remaining ½ teaspoon each salt and pepper, and the Asiago to the pasta. Toss until well combined.

Divide the linguine among serving plates and top each with 2 of the shrimp skewers. Serve hot.

1 pound large shrimp, shelled & deveined

1 pint cherry tomatoes

¼ cup plus 1 tablespoon extra-virgin olive oil

1 teaspoon salt

1 teaspoon freshly ground pepper

1 pound imported linguine

½ cup chopped fresh flat-leaf parsley

⅓ cup chopped fresh basil

2 tablespoons chopped fresh mint

1 tablespoon chopped fresh rosemary

½ cup freshly grated Asiago cheese

# PASTA WITH GRILLED

*Serves 4 to 6*

**For any vegetarian, this dish can become a staple. Look for eggplants that are long, slender, and very firm.**

SPRINKLE THE EGGPLANT SLICES with 1½ teaspoons of the salt. Put into a large bowl and set aside for 1 hour.

In a large serving bowl, combine the tomatoes, basil, olives, garlic, the remaining ¼ teaspoon salt, the red pepper flakes, and 2 tablespoons of the oil, tossing well. Set aside.

Preheat the grill to high and brush with oil.

Pat the eggplant slices dry and brush with the remaining 2 tablespoons oil. Grill the eggplant, in batches, for 2 to 3 minutes on each side, or until browned and tender. Remove to a cutting board, and when cool enough to handle, coarsely chop and add to the tomato mixture.

Meanwhile, bring a large pot of water to a rolling boil and add salt to taste. Cook the bow ties according to the package directions, until al dente. Drain well.

Add the pasta to the vegetables and sprinkle with the Parmesan, tossing until well mixed. Serve hot.

---

- **2 medium-size eggplants (about 1 pound each), cut lengthwise in half & then crosswise into ¼-inch-thick slices**
- **1¾ teaspoons salt**
- **One 28-ounce can whole tomatoes, drained, seeded & chopped**
- **½ cup packed julienned fresh basil**
- **⅓ cup chopped pitted Kalamata or Gaeta olives**
- **1 large garlic clove, minced**
- **¼ teaspoon crushed red pepper flakes**
- **¼ cup extra-virgin olive oil**
- **1 pound bow ties (farfalle)**
- **½ cup freshly grated Parmesan cheese**

# SUMMER VEGETABLES

## FUSILLI WITH

Here's a colorful pasta dish that can be made several hours ahead of time. Cook the pasta a little less than you normally would, since it will soften up a bit as it sits. The flavor tends to mellow as well, so adjust the seasoning just before serving.

*serves 4*

PREHEAT THE GRILL to high and brush with oil.

Grill the bell peppers, turning them, for about 15 minutes, or until blackened. Transfer to a paper bag and let steam for 10 minutes. When cool enough to handle, peel, core, seed, and cut into large pieces.

In a food processor, combine the bell peppers, basil, anchovies, garlic, 2 tablespoons of the oil, the vinegars, and ½ teaspoon of the salt and ½ teaspoon of the pepper. Process, pulsing, until finely chopped. Set aside.

Put the vegetables on a baking sheet. Brush with the remaining 3 tablespoons oil, and sprinkle with ¾ teaspoon each salt and pepper.

Grill the vegetables, turning them, for 5 to 10 minutes, or until tender. Remove to a cutting board, cut the vegetables crosswise into ½-inch-wide strips, and add to the bowl.

Meanwhile, bring a large pot of salted water to a boil. Cook the pasta until al dente; drain. Transfer to the serving bowl.

Pour the red pepper sauce over the pasta and toss until mixed. Sprinkle with the Romano and serve hot or warm.

2 red bell peppers

½ cup loosely packed fresh basil leaves

4 anchovy fillets, coarsely chopped

1 small garlic clove, minced

¼ cup plus 1 tablespoon extra-virgin olive oil

2 tablespoons red wine vinegar

2 tablespoons balsamic vinegar

1¼ teaspoons salt

1¼ teaspoons freshly ground pepper

1 large eggplant (about 1½ pounds), washed & cut lengthwise into ½-inch-thick slices

1 medium-size fennel bulb (about 1 pound), trimmed & cut lengthwise into ¼-inch-thick slices, feathery tops reserved

2 medium-size yellow squash (about 8 ounces), cut lengthwise into ¼-inch-thick slices

2 medium-size zucchini (about 8 ounces), cut lengthwise into ¼-inch-thick slices

1 pound fusilli

½ cup freshly grated Pecorino Romano cheese

*Serves 4*

**Pancetta is unsmoked cured bacon available in Italian specialty stores and in some grocery stores. If you can't find pancetta, substitute five slices of bacon, but blanch them in boiling water for one minute before grilling.**

PREHEAT THE GRILL to high and brush with oil.

In a large shallow dish, toss the asparagus with 1 tablespoon of the oil, ¼ teaspoon of the salt, and ¼ teaspoon of the pepper.

Grill the asparagus, turning several times, for 3 to 5 minutes, or until browned and tender. Remove and set aside. Grill the pancetta for 1 to 2 minutes on each side, or until golden. Remove and set aside.

Cut the asparagus into 1½-inch lengths and put into a large serving dish. Coarsely chop the pancetta and add to the bowl along with the parsley, onion, sage, garlic, lemon zest, lemon juice, the remaining ½ teaspoon each salt and pepper, and the remaining 3 tablespoons oil. Toss until well mixed.

Meanwhile, bring a large pot of water to a rolling boil over high heat and add salt to taste. Cook the penne according to package directions until al dente. Reserve ¼ cup of the pasta water and drain the penne.

Add the reserved pasta water and the penne to the bowl with the asparagus, tossing until combined. Sprinkle with the Parmesan and serve hot.

**2 pounds thin asparagus, tough ends removed**

**¼ cup extra-virgin olive oil**

**¾ teaspoon salt**

**¾ teaspoon freshly ground pepper**

**¼ pound sliced pancetta**

**½ cup chopped fresh flat-leaf parsley**

**¼ cup finely chopped red onion**

**1 tablespoon chopped fresh sage**

**1 small garlic clove, mashed to a paste**

**1 teaspoon grated lemon zest**

**2 tablespoons fresh lemon juice**

**1 pound penne**

**½ cup freshly grated Parmesan cheese**

# POLENTA WITH WILD

*Serves 4 to 6*

There may be plenty of people who can spend forty minutes making polenta the old-fashioned way, but you do not really need to. Here's my recipe for fast polenta.

PREHEAT THE GRILL to high, set a vegetable grill rack on top, and brush with oil.

Prepare the mushrooms: Grill the mushrooms in batches, turning occasionally, for 2 to 5 minutes, or until browned and softened, removing them to a large bowl as they are cooked. Add the oil, salt, and pepper and toss to coat evenly. Cover to keep warm.

Prepare the polenta: In a medium-size heavy-bottomed saucepan, bring the milk, water, parsley, rosemary, and salt to a boil over high heat. Whisking constantly in one direction, slowly add the polenta. Reduce the heat to low and cook, stirring constantly with a wooden spoon, for 2 to 4 minutes, or until the polenta has thickened. Divide among large shallow bowls and top with the mushrooms. Sprinkle with the basil and Romano and serve hot.

## MUSHROOMS

- 1 pound cremini mushrooms, briefly rinsed, trimmed & quartered
- 1 pound mixed mushrooms such as chanterelle, oyster, hedgehog, and/or morel, briefly rinsed, trimmed & cut into ½-inch pieces
- 2 tablespoons extra-virgin olive oil
- ½ teaspoon salt
- ½ teaspoon freshly ground pepper

## POLENTA

- 5 cups 2% milk
- 2 cups water
- ¼ cup chopped fresh flat-leaf parsley
- 1 tablespoon chopped fresh rosemary
- 2 teaspoons salt
- 2 cups imported instant polenta (about 12 ounces)

- ⅓ cup chopped fresh basil
- ⅓ cup freshly grated Pecorino Romano cheese

# PENNE WITH TUNA & PEPPERS

Serves 4

When green bell peppers are grilled, their acidity disappears and they become sweet and tender. Here, tuna is combined with green, red, and yellow bell peppers. Roasted poblano pepper gives the dish the feel of southern California.

PREHEAT THE GRILL to high and brush with oil.

Grill the bell peppers and the poblano chile, turning occasionally, for about 15 minutes, or until blackened. Transfer to a paper bag and let steam for 10 minutes. When cool enough to handle, peel, core, and seed the bell peppers and poblano chile. Cut into ¼-inch-wide strips and put in a large serving bowl.

Add the tomatoes, 3 tablespoons of the oil, the parsley, capers, garlic, ½ teaspoon of the salt, and ½ teaspoon of the pepper. Toss until combined and set aside.

Brush the tuna with the remaining 1 tablespoon oil, and sprinkle with the remaining ½ teaspoon each salt and pepper.

Grill the tuna for 1 to 2 minutes on each side, or until just light pink in the center. Cut into 1-inch chunks and add to the vegetables. Cover to keep warm.

Meanwhile, bring a large pot of water to a rolling boil and add salt to taste. Cook the penne according to the package directions until al dente. Drain well.

Add the pasta to the vegetables, toss gently to combine, and serve hot or at room temperature.

2 red bell peppers

1 yellow bell pepper

1 green bell pepper

1 poblano chile

6 canned whole tomatoes, drained, seeded & chopped

¼ cup extra-virgin olive oil

¼ cup chopped fresh flat-leaf parsley

2 tablespoons capers

1 garlic clove, minced

1 teaspoon salt

1 teaspoon freshly ground pepper

¾ pound tuna steak, about ½-inch thick

1 pound penne

# VEGETABLES & SALADS

# ARTICHOKES

## MINT-STUFFED

The flavors of this dish are inspired by the classic braised Roman artichokes which are cooked slowly with lots of olive oil, mint, and garlic. The same ingredients are used here, but grilling imparts a smoky flavor that enriches the flavor of the artichokes. If the artichokes you purchase are thornless, there will be no need to trim off the tops of the leaves.

PREHEAT THE GRILL to medium and brush with oil.

Using your fingers, snap back and remove the outer leaves from the artichokes, including any that are bruised. Using a sharp knife, trim about 1 inch off the tops of the artichokes. With kitchen scissors, snip off the tops of the remaining outer leaves. Cut the artichokes in half. With the tip of a teaspoon, remove the hairy chokes and discard.

Put 1 inch of water and ½ teaspoon of the salt into a large nonreactive pot. Add the artichokes, cover, and cook for 10 to 12 minutes, or until the artichoke bottoms are tender when pierced with a small knife. Using tongs, remove the artichokes and drain well.

In a small bowl, combine the mint, garlic, oil, lemon juice, the remaining ½ teaspoon salt, and the pepper. Using a small spoon, stuff the mint mixture between the leaves of the artichokes, dividing it evenly. Grill the artichokes for about 3 to 4 minutes on each side, or until nicely browned. Transfer to a dish and serve hot or warm.

4 medium-size artichokes, stems trimmed & peeled

1 teaspoon salt

3 tablespoons chopped fresh mint

1 garlic clove, minced

2 tablespoons extra-virgin olive oil

1 tablespoon fresh lemon juice

½ teaspoon freshly ground pepper

*Serves 4*

**P**REHEAT THE GRILL to high.

In a large bowl, toss the asparagus with the oil. Grill the asparagus, turning once or twice, for 5 to 10 minutes depending upon the thickness of the spears, until browned and tender. Remove to a serving platter and sprinkle with the basil, salt, and pepper. Top with the Parmesan shavings and serve.

When grilled, asparagus develops a rich woodsy flavor. Here it's presented very simply, with just a sprinkling of oil, basil, and salt. To gild the lily a bit, sprinkle a few Parmesan shavings on top.

1½ pounds asparagus, tough ends removed

1½ tablespoons extra-virgin olive oil

3 tablespoons chopped fresh basil

½ teaspoon kosher salt

½ teaspoon freshly ground pepper

Parmesan shavings (removed with a vegetable peeler)

# WITH ANCHOVY SAUCE

**If your eating audience like anchovies and eggplant, this recipe will indeed impress. Fanned and grilled baby eggplants are amazing to look at, and tender and flavorful to eat.**

*Serves 4*

CUT THE EGGPLANTS INTO FANS by making ¼-inch-thick lengthwise cuts beginning at the bottom ends and cutting towards the stem ends, leaving the stems intact. Press down with the heel of your hand at the stem end of each eggplant to gently fan the slices. Lightly brush the eggplants with 1 tablespoon of the oil and sprinkle with the salt and pepper.

Preheat the grill to high and brush with oil.

In a small bowl, combine the anchovies, parsley, garlic, vinegar, and the remaining 2 tablespoons oil, whisking until mixed. Set the anchovy sauce aside.

Grill the eggplant, turning once, for 10 to 12 minutes, or until tender. Transfer to a serving platter, drizzle with the anchovy sauce, and sprinkle with the walnuts. Serve the eggplant hot or warm.

8 baby eggplants (about 1½ pounds)

3 tablespoons extra-virgin olive oil

½ teaspoon salt

½ teaspoon freshly ground pepper

4 anchovy fillets, minced

2 teaspoons chopped fresh flat-leaf parsley

1 small garlic clove, minced

1 tablespoon red wine vinegar

2 tablespoons toasted walnuts, finely chopped

*Serves 4*

This is an unusual and pretty presentation for Belgian endive. Grilling endive tames its bitterness considerably, and its flavor melds nicely with the saltiness of the capers and the olives.

PREHEAT THE GRILL to high and brush with oil.

In a small bowl, combine the scallions, tomato, olives, capers, lemon juice, 2 tablespoons of the oil, ¼ teaspoon of the salt, and ¼ teaspoon of the pepper. Set aside.

Brush the endive with the remaining 1 tablespoon oil, and sprinkle with the remaining ¼ teaspoon each salt and pepper. Grill the endive, turning once, for about 6 minutes, or until browned and tender. Remove to a serving platter, drizzle with the dressing, and serve warm.

- 2 scallions, finely chopped
- 2 tablespoons finely chopped tomato
- 2 tablespoons chopped pitted oil-cured black olives
- 1 tablespoon capers, rinsed
- 1 teaspoon fresh lemon juice
- 3 tablespoons extra-virgin olive oil
- ½ teaspoon salt
- ½ teaspoon freshly ground pepper
- 4 heads Belgian endive, cut lengthwise into quarters

# GOAT CHEESE SALAD

*Serves 4*

**Grilled fennel is one of my very favorite foods. Here, its sweetness combines with spicy arugula and tart goat cheese to make a delicious salad. When buying fennel, look for bulbs that are white and plump.**

PREHEAT THE GRILL to medium-hot and brush with oil.

Brush the fennel with 1 tablespoon of the oil. Sprinkle with ¼ teaspoon of the salt and ¼ teaspoon of the pepper. Grill for 2 to 3 minutes on each side, or until tender. Remove the fennel from the grill and set aside.

In a large bowl, combine the remaining 2 tablespoons oil, the lemon juice, and the remaining ¼ teaspoon each salt and pepper. Add the arugula, tossing to coat. Place the arugula on serving plates. Top with the grilled fennel and sprinkle with the goat cheese. Serve immediately.

2 large fennel bulbs, trimmed
& cut lengthwise into
¼-inch-thick slices

3 tablespoons olive oil

½ teaspoon salt

½ teaspoon freshly ground
pepper

1 tablespoon fresh lemon
juice

2 large bunches arugula,
trimmed & washed

2 tablespoons crumbled
goat cheese

# MEDITERRANEAN

*Serves 4*

Here's a plate of smoky grilled fennel, lightly dressed with a refreshing orange, parsley, and garlic vinaigrette—very Mediterranean, and very summery.

P REHEAT THE GRILL to high. Set a vegetable grill rack on top and brush with oil.

In a small saucepan, bring the orange juice to a boil over high heat. Boil for about 8 minutes, or until reduced to ⅓ cup. Remove from the heat and whisk in 1 tablespoon of the oil, the parsley, garlic, salt, and pepper. Keep warm over very low heat.

Brush the fennel with the remaining 1 tablespoon oil. Grill, turning once, for about 5 minutes, or until browned and tender. Transfer to a serving platter and drizzle with the orange sauce. Serve the fennel hot or warm.

1 cup fresh orange juice

2 tablespoons extra-virgin olive oil

2 tablespoons chopped fresh flat-leaf parsley

1 small garlic clove, minced

¼ teaspoon salt

¼ teaspoon freshly ground pepper

4 fennel bulbs, trimmed, halved & thinly sliced lengthwise

# ARUGULA PESTO

**Prepare this in late summer when leeks are newly harvested and somewhat more reasonable in price. Wash them very carefully (biting down on leek grit is unpleasant), and save the braising broth for soup.**

PREHEAT THE GRILL to high and brush with oil.

Put the leeks into a large skillet and add the chicken broth and enough water to barely cover the leeks. Add ½ teaspoon of the salt and ½ teaspoon of the pepper, and bring to a boil over high heat. Cover, reduce the heat to medium-low, and simmer for about 10 minutes, or until the leeks are very tender. Remove the leeks to a platter, reserving the broth.

In a food processor or blender, combine the arugula, parsley, walnuts, garlic, 2 tablespoons of the oil, the lemon juice, and the remaining ¼ teaspoon each salt and pepper. Process to a coarse puree. With the machine running, gradually add ¼ cup of the reserved leek broth, processing until blended. Pour into a serving bowl and set aside.

Brush the leeks with the remaining 1 tablespoon oil. Grill the leeks, turning once, for about 2 minutes on each side, or until browned. Transfer to a small platter and serve with the pesto.

8 large leeks, trimmed to 8-inch lengths, halved lengthwise & thoroughly washed

2 cups chicken broth

¾ teaspoon salt

¾ teaspoon freshly ground pepper

1 large bunch arugula, trimmed, washed & coarsely chopped

¼ cup fresh flat-leaf parsley leaves

2 tablespoons chopped walnuts

1 small garlic clove, chopped

3 tablespoons extra-virgin olive oil

2 teaspoons fresh lemon juice

# SUMMER VEGETABLE SALAD

*Serves 4*

In this recipe I've given a suggested list of vegetables, but use whatever looks best at the market. Serve this to vegetarians and they will be very, very happy.

PREHEAT THE GRILL to high. Set a vegetable grill rack on top and brush with oil.

Grill the peppers, turning them, for about 15 minutes, or until blackened on all sides. Transfer to a paper bag and let steam for 10 minutes. When the peppers are cool enough to handle, peel, core, and seed them, then cut into quarters. Set aside.

Meanwhile, put the eggplant, scallions, fennel, squash, and mushrooms on a baking sheet. Brush with ¼ cup of the oil and sprinkle with 1 teaspoon of the salt and 1 teaspoon of the pepper.

Grill the vegetables, in batches, for 2 to 4 minutes on each side, or until browned and tender. Remove to a serving platter.

Meanwhile, in a small food processor, process the garlic and the remaining ¼ teaspoon salt until a paste forms. Add the basil and the remaining ¼ teaspoon pepper and process, pulsing, until the basil is finely chopped. With the motor running, slowly add the remaining ¼ cup oil. Transfer to a bowl or serving dish and stir in the Parmesan.

Drizzle the pesto over the vegetables, or serve alongside as a dip.

1 yellow bell pepper

1 red bell pepper

1 small eggplant (about 1 pound), cut lengthwise into ½-inch-thick slices

1 bunch scallions, trimmed

1 fennel bulb, trimmed & thinly sliced lengthwise

4 baby pattypan squash or 2 small zucchini, cut lengthwise into ½-inch-thick slices

2 portobello mushrooms, stems removed, briefly rinsed & cut into ½-inch-thick slices

½ cup extra-virgin olive oil

1¼ teaspoons salt

1¼ teaspoons freshly ground pepper

1 garlic clove, chopped

1 cup packed fresh basil leaves

¼ cup freshly grated Parmesan cheese

# STUFFED RADICCHIO

## MOZZARELLA-

Radicchio can be bitter in its uncooked state. But grill it, and you have a completely different vegetable—radicchio that is mild and tender. Stuff the radicchio wedges with smoked mozzarella slices and drizzle with a pungent basil anchovy sauce, and you have a great amalgamation of flavors.

PREHEAT THE GRILL to high and brush with oil.

Place 2 slices of the mozzarella between the leaves of each radicchio wedge, spacing the cheese evenly.

In a small bowl, combine the oil, basil, anchovies, and pepper. Set aside.

Grill the radicchio, turning occasionally, for about 5 minutes, until it is wilted and lightly browned on all sides, and the cheese has begun to melt. Transfer to a serving platter, drizzle with the basil anchovy sauce, and serve.

Sixteen 1-x-2-inch very thin slices smoked mozzarella cheese (about 8 ounces)

2 large heads radicchio, each cut into 4 wedges

2 tablespoons extra-virgin olive oil

2 tablespoons chopped fresh basil

3 anchovy fillets, finely chopped

¼ teaspoon freshly ground pepper

# PORTOBELLOS WITH

*Serves 6*

PREHEAT THE GRILL to high and brush with oil.

In a small saucepan, combine the rosemary, garlic, and oil over high heat. When the oil begins to simmer, reduce the heat to medium-low and cook for 2 to 3 minutes, or until the garlic is golden. Pour the oil through a strainer into a small bowl. Discard the garlic and set the rosemary and oil aside.

Brush the mushrooms with some of the rosemary oil. Grill the mushrooms for about 4 minutes on each side, or until browned and tender. Transfer, cap side up, to a serving dish and drizzle with the remaining rosemary oil. Sprinkle with the tomato, the reserved rosemary, salt, and pepper. Serve hot or warm.

Portobellos are actually mature cremini mushrooms. When grilled, they develop a meaty texture and an earthy taste. The rosemary is simmered in oil until crispy and becomes an interesting texture contrast to the tender mushrooms.

⅓ cup fresh rosemary

3 garlic cloves, thinly sliced

¼ cup extra-virgin olive oil

6 portobello mushrooms (4 to 5 inches in diameter), stems removed & briefly rinsed

1 plum tomato, halved, seeded & finely chopped

½ teaspoon salt

½ teaspoon freshly ground pepper

# GRILLED MUSHROOM

*Serves 4*

PREHEAT THE GRILL to high, set a vegetable grill rack on top, and brush with oil.

Grill the bread for about 1 minute on each side, or until lightly toasted. Brush with about 1 tablespoon of the oil and keep warm.

Grill the mushrooms for 5 to 6 minutes, or until browned and tender. Transfer to a large bowl and add the tomato, parsley, basil, the porcini if using, the remaining oil, the vinegar, salt, and pepper, tossing to mix. Set aside about ½ cup of the mushroom mixture.

Place 1 slice of the bread on each serving plate. Spoon half the mushroom mixture on the bread, dividing it evenly. Cover each with a second slice of bread and top with the remaining mushrooms. Cover with the remaining slices of bread and top with the reserved mushroom mixture. Garnish with the Asiago cheese shavings and serve immediately.

If you can't find shiitake mushrooms, substitute button or additional cremini mushrooms instead. To prevent the mushrooms from falling into the coals, use a vegetable grill rack.

Twelve 4-x-3-x ¼-inch slices country bread

3 tablespoons extra-virgin olive oil

½ pound medium-size cremini mushrooms, briefly rinsed, trimmed & halved

½ pound medium-size shiitake mushrooms, stems removed, briefly rinsed & halved

1 large tomato, chopped

3 tablespoons chopped fresh flat-leaf parsley

1 tablespoon chopped fresh basil

¼ teaspoon finely grated dried porcini mushroom (optional)

1 tablespoon red wine vinegar

½ teaspoon salt

½ teaspoon freshly ground pepper

¼ cup Asiago cheese shavings (removed with a vegetable peeler), for garnish

# PANZANELLA

*Serves 6*

**There are probably a million recipes for panzanella, the traditional Tuscan bread salad. This one has a new twist, since it involves grilling the vegetables as well as the bread.**

PREHEAT THE GRILL to high and brush with oil.

Grill the bread for 1 to 2 minutes on each side, or until lightly toasted. Set aside.

Grill the peppers, turning several times, for about 10 minutes, or until blackened on all sides. Transfer the peppers to a paper bag and let steam for 10 minutes. When cool enough to handle, peel, core, seed, and coarsely chop the peppers.

While the peppers are cooling, grill the onion slices, turning once, for about 5 minutes, or until browned. When cool enough to handle, coarsely chop the onion. Put the onion and peppers in a large bowl.

Cut the bread into ¾-inch cubes and put into the bowl. Add the remaining ingredients and toss well to mix. Set the panzanella aside at room temperature for 30 minutes to allow the flavors to develop.

To serve, toss the salad again lightly and transfer to a serving bowl.

Four ¾-inch-thick large slices country bread

2 yellow bell peppers

1 medium-size red onion, cut into ½-inch-thick slices

3 large tomatoes, coarsely chopped

1½ cups chopped English cucumber

3 tablespoons capers

2 tablespoons extra-virgin olive oil

1 tablespoon red wine vinegar, or more to taste

1 teaspoon salt

½ teaspoon freshly ground pepper

# ORANGE & HERBS

**Peeling roasted peppers has got to be one of the messier jobs in the kitchen, but it is worth it. Here's my method: once the peppers have steamed for ten minutes in a paper bag, rip the bag open so it lies flat. Peel, seed, and core the peppers right on the bag. Then roll up the bag, mess and all, and discard— or throw on the compost heap if you have one.**

PREHEAT THE GRILL to high and brush with oil.

Grill the peppers, turning several times, for about 10 minutes, or until blackened on all sides. Transfer to a paper bag and let steam for 10 minutes. When the peppers are cool enough to handle, peel, core, and seed them. Cut into ½-inch-wide strips and put into a medium-size bowl. Set aside.

In a small bowl, combine the oil, parsley, thyme, oregano, garlic, orange zest, salt, and pepper, whisking until mixed. Pour over the peppers and toss until well coated. Transfer to a serving dish.

2 red bell peppers

2 yellow bell peppers

2 green, purple, or orange bell peppers

3 tablespoons extra-virgin olive oil

2 tablespoons chopped fresh flat-leaf parsley

1 tablespoon chopped fresh thyme

½ teaspoon dried oregano, crumbled

1 garlic clove, minced

1 teaspoon grated orange zest

½ teaspoon salt

½ teaspoon freshly ground pepper

# RED ONION SALAD

*Serves 4*

**This is an opportunity to splurge with a good-quality balsamic vinegar. It makes an incredible difference. To shave the cheese, use a vegetable peeler.**

PREHEAT THE GRILL to high. Set a vegetable grill rack on top and brush with oil. Grill the onions for about 5 minutes on each side, or until softened and browned. Transfer the onions to a large bowl.

When the onions are cool enough to handle, separate into rings. Add the mint, vinegar, oil, salt, and pepper, tossing until mixed. Transfer to a small platter and sprinkle with the Romano cheese shavings. Serve hot or warm.

**2 large red onions (about 1 pound each), cut into ½-inch-thick slices**

**2 large sweet onions such as Walla Wallas or Vidalias (about 1 pound each), cut into ½-inch-thick slices**

**3 tablespoons chopped fresh mint**

**1 tablespoon plus 1 teaspoon balsamic vinegar**

**1 tablespoon extra-virgin olive oil**

**½ teaspoon salt**

**½ teaspoon freshly ground pepper**

**⅓ cup Pecorino Romano cheese shavings**

# NEW POTATOES WITH ROSEMARY

*Serves 4*

Potatoes seem to be made for the combination of rosemary and salt. Here, they get nicely browned and crispy on the grill. If you don't have red potatoes, any waxy or boiling potato will work fine.

PREHEAT THE GRILL to medium-high and brush with oil.

In a medium-size saucepan, cover the potatoes with cold salted water and bring to a boil over high heat. Reduce the heat to medium and cook for 8 to 10 minutes, or until just cooked through. Drain thoroughly.

In a large bowl, toss the potatoes with the rosemary, garlic, salt, pepper, and oil. Grill the potatoes for 2 to 3 minutes on each side, or until browned. Transfer to a serving dish, sprinkle with the lemon zest, and serve.

1½ pounds small red-skinned potatoes, scrubbed & halved

2 tablespoons chopped fresh rosemary

1 small garlic clove, minced

¾ teaspoon salt

½ teaspoon freshly ground pepper

1½ tablespoons extra-virgin olive oil

2 teaspoons grated lemon zest

# TOMATO SALAD

*Serves 4*

**This is one of those great dishes that was born for entertaining. It can be made completely ahead of time and is gorgeous to behold. And, if you have any left over, which is doubtful, it makes a great sandwich on a baguette or roll.**

PREHEAT THE GRILL to high and brush with oil.

Grill the peppers, turning them several times, for 15 minutes, or until blackened on all sides. Transfer to a paper bag and let steam for 10 minutes. When the peppers are cool enough to handle, peel, core, and seed them. Cut the peppers into 1-inch-wide strips. Set aside.

Grill the tomato halves for about 1 minute on each side, or until lightly charred. Transfer to a serving platter. Scatter the pepper strips around the tomatoes. Sprinkle with the salt and pepper and drizzle with the oil. Sprinkle with the capers, parsley, and marjoram, and top with the ricotta salata and olives. Serve at room temperature.

2 red bell peppers

2 yellow bell peppers

6 plum tomatoes, halved

¼ teaspoon salt

½ teaspoon freshly ground pepper

1½ tablespoons extra-virgin olive oil

1 tablespoon capers

1 tablespoon chopped fresh flat-leaf parsley

1 teaspoon chopped fresh marjoram

3 tablespoons crumbled ricotta salata or feta cheese

½ cup oil-cured black olives

# GRILLED TOMATOES

**These tomatoes are amazingly good and so easy to make. You simply top plum tomatoes with smoked mozzarella and thyme, and grill them. If you can find lemon thyme or lemon balm, use it in place of the thyme.**

*Serves 4*

PREHEAT THE GRILL to high and brush with oil.

Sprinkle the cut side of the tomatoes with the salt and pepper. Top with the mozzarella and sprinkle with the parsley and thyme.

Place the tomatoes, cut side up, on the grill. Cover and grill for 3 to 4 minutes, or until the cheese melts. Transfer to a serving dish and serve hot or warm.

6 plum tomatoes, halved & seeded

½ teaspoon salt

½ teaspoon freshly ground pepper

¾ cup grated smoked mozzarella cheese

1 tablespoon chopped fresh flat-leaf parsley

1 tablespoon chopped fresh thyme

# YELLOW SQUASH WITH

*Serves 4*

**I made this dish after finding some brilliant, neon yellow summer squash at a farmer's market. Their color faded a bit during cooking, but since the squash were quite small, they were deliciously sweet and tender.**

PREHEAT THE GRILL to high and brush with oil.

With a large knife, chop the parsley, mint, and garlic together until very finely minced. Set aside.

Brush the squash slices on both sides with 1 tablespoon of the oil and sprinkle with the salt and pepper. Grill for 3 to 4 minutes on each side, until nicely marked and tender. Remove to a platter, sprinkle with the herb mixture, and drizzle with the remaining ½ tablespoon oil. Serve hot or at room temperature.

**2 tablespoons coarsely chopped fresh flat-leaf parsley**

**1 tablespoon coarsely chopped fresh mint**

**1 small garlic clove**

**1½ pounds small yellow squash, cut lengthwise into ¼-inch-thick slices**

**1½ tablespoons extra-virgin olive oil**

**½ teaspoon salt**

**½ teaspoon freshly ground pepper**

# TOASTED PIGNOLI

**Here's a pretty dish of grilled zucchini dressed with toasted pignoli, Parmesan shavings, lemon zest, and herbs.**

*Serves 4*

PREHEAT THE GRILL to high and brush with oil.

Toast the pignoli in a small skillet over medium-high heat for about 2 minutes, or until lightly browned. Transfer to a small dish and let cool. Add the basil, rosemary, and lemon zest, tossing until mixed. Set aside.

Brush the zucchini with the oil and sprinkle with the salt and pepper. Grill for 2 to 3 minutes on each side, or until browned and tender. Transfer to a serving platter, sprinkle with the pignoli mixture and the Parmesan shavings, and serve.

2 tablespoons pignoli (pine nuts)

2 tablespoons julienned fresh basil

1 teaspoon chopped fresh rosemary

½ teaspoon grated lemon zest

5 medium-size zucchini (about 1¼ pounds), cut lengthwise into ¼-inch-thick slices

2 tablespoons extra-virgin olive oil

½ teaspoon salt

½ teaspoon freshly ground pepper

¼ cup Parmesan cheese shavings (removed with a vegetable peeler)

# PIZZA, BRUSCHETTA & PANINI

# MARGHERITA

*Serves 4*

When you're making pizza, don't worry about shaping it into a perfect circle. Just roll the dough out as evenly as possible without any major holes. I think it looks really great free-form, very Jackson Pollack, with the melted cheese and red and yellow tomatoes sprinkled all over.

PREHEAT THE GRILL to high and brush with oil.

Lightly flour 2 baking sheets. On a lightly floured surface, roll one piece of dough into a circle about ⅛ inch thick. Place on a prepared baking sheet. Roll out the remaining dough and place on the baking sheets.

Place one piece of the dough on the grill. Grill for about 1 minute, or until the underside of the dough is nicely browned. Using tongs, turn the dough over and grill for about 30 seconds, until the underside just stiffens. Transfer to a baking sheet and repeat with the remaining dough rounds.

Brush the pizzas with the oil. Spread the tomatoes evenly over the crusts and sprinkle with the mozzarella, Romano, garlic, and salt. Top with the basil. Grill the pizzas, covered, 1 or 2 at a time, for 2 to 3 minutes, or until the cheese melts, making sure the undersides of the pizzas don't burn.

1 recipe Pizza Dough (page 88), divided into 4 pieces

2 tablespoons extra-virgin olive oil

2 cups peeled, seeded & chopped plum tomatoes or one 28-ounce can whole tomatoes, drained, seeded & chopped

1 cup grated fresh mozzarella or Italian Fontina cheese (4 ounces)

¼ cup freshly grated Pecorino Romano cheese

1 garlic clove, minced

½ teaspoon salt

1 cup lightly packed fresh basil leaves

# PIZZA DOUGH

I always add a bit of whole wheat flour to my dough—it adds body and sweetness. If desired, prepare the dough the night before or in the morning and let it rise in the refrigerator. The dough can also be prepared up to two days ahead—place in a bowl, cover with plastic wrap, and refrigerate.

*Enough dough for 4 individual pizzas*

IN A SMALL BOWL, stir together the water, oil, yeast, and sugar. Let stand for about 5 minutes, or until bubbly. In a food processor, combine the all-purpose flour, whole-wheat flour, and salt. Pulse to mix. With the motor running, pour in the yeast mixture, and process, pulsing, for 2 minutes.

On a lightly floured surface, briefly knead the dough. (The dough will be somewhat sticky.) Place in a large oiled bowl, turning the dough to coat with oil. Cover and let rise in a warm place for 2 to 3 hours, or until doubled in volume.

Alternatively, to make the dough by hand, in a large bowl, stir together the water, oil, yeast, and sugar. Let stand for about 5 minutes, or until bubbly. In a medium-size bowl, stir together the all-purpose flour, whole-wheat flour, and salt. Using a wooden spoon, stir the flour mixture into the yeast mixture, stirring until a sticky dough forms. On a lightly floured surface, knead the dough for several minutes, until smooth and less sticky. Place in a large oiled bowl, turning to coat with oil. Cover and let rise in a warm place for 2 to 3 hours, or until doubled in volume.

1½ cups warm water (105° to 115°F)

1 tablespoon extra-virgin olive oil

1 envelope active dry yeast

1 teaspoon sugar

4 cups all-purpose flour

⅔ cup whole-wheat flour

1½ teaspoons salt

*Serves 4*

Pizza is one dish that thrives on improvisation. Use a combination of flavors, colors, and textures. it's hard to go wrong.

PREHEAT THE GRILL to high. Set a vegetable grill rack on top and brush with oil.

Grill the bell pepper, turning, for about 15 minutes, or until blackened. Transfer to a paper bag and let steam for 10 minutes. When cool, peel, core, and seed. Cut the pepper into ¼-inch-wide strips and put into a medium-size bowl. Add the tomatoes, 1 tablespoon of the oil, the parsley, garlic, and ¼ teaspoon each salt and pepper; mix.

In another bowl, toss the shrimp with 1 tablespoon of the remaining oil and the remaining ¼ teaspoon each salt and pepper. Grill for 30 seconds on each side, or until firm to the touch. Set aside. Grill the onion slices for 3 minutes on each side, or until browned. Set aside. Remove the vegetable grill rack.

Follow the directions for shaping the pizzas on page 86. Place one piece of dough on the grill. Grill for about 1 minute, or until the underside is nicely browned. Turn and grill for about 30 seconds, or until the underside is just stiffened. Transfer to a baking sheet and repeat with the remaining dough.

Brush the pizzas with the remaining 1 tablespoon oil. Top with the bell pepper mixture, shrimp, onions, and Fontina. Grill until the cheese melts.

1 yellow bell pepper

6 canned whole tomatoes, halved, seeded & chopped

3 tablespoons extra-virgin olive oil

½ cup chopped fresh flat-leaf parsley

1 garlic clove, minced

½ teaspoon salt

½ teaspoon freshly ground pepper

½ pound medium-size shrimp, peeled & deveined

1 large red onion, cut into ¼-inch-thick slices

1 recipe Pizza Dough (page 88), divided into 4 pieces

2 cups grated Italian Fontina cheese (8 ounces)

# GARLIC-POTATO PIZZA

**ROASTED**

**Many people think the combination of potatoes and pizza is a little strange. I think it's a great carbohydrate mix, especially when the pizza is spiked with fresh rosemary, roasted garlic, and smoked mozzarella.**

PREHEAT THE OVEN to 400°F.

Wrap the garlic tightly in foil and roast for about 1 hour, or until very soft when gently pressed. When cool, squeeze out the garlic pulp from the cloves and mash. Combine the garlic, oil, rosemary, ¼ teaspoon of the salt, and the red pepper flakes in a small bowl. Preheat the grill to high and brush with oil.

Put the potatoes in a saucepan and add cold water to cover and the remaining 1 teaspoon salt. Bring to a boil over high heat, then reduce the heat and simmer for 15 minutes, or until tender. Drain, and when cool, slice as thinly as possible. Set aside.

Follow the directions for shaping the pizzas on page 86. Place one piece of dough on the grill. Grill for about 1 minute, or until the underside is nicely browned. Turn the dough over and grill for 30 seconds, or until stiffened. Transfer to a baking sheet and repeat with the remaining dough rounds.

Brush the crusts with the garlic mixture. Arrange the potato slices on top and sprinkle with the mozzarella cheeses. Grill the pizzas, 1 or 2 at a time, for 2 to 3 minutes, or until the cheese is melted.

---

2 large heads garlic, papery outer skin removed & the top 1 inch cut off

3 tablespoons extra-virgin olive oil

1 tablespoon chopped fresh rosemary

1¼ teaspoons salt

¼ to ½ teaspoon crushed red pepper flakes

1 pound medium-size red-skinned potatoes, scrubbed

1 recipe Pizza Dough (page 88), divided into 4 pieces

2 cups grated smoked mozzarella cheese (8 ounces)

1 cup grated mozzarella cheese (4 ounces)

# EGGPLANT & GOAT

*Serves 4*

**P**REHEAT THE GRILL to high and brush with oil.

Lightly brush the eggplant with 1 to 2 tablespoons basil oil and sprinkle with ½ teaspoon of the salt and ½ teaspoon of the pepper. Grill, turning once, for about 5 minutes on each side, or until browned and tender. Remove and set aside.

Sprinkle the tomatoes with the remaining ¼ teaspoon each salt and pepper. Grill, turning once, for about 3 minutes on each side, or until charred and softened. Remove to a cutting board and coarsely chop. Set aside.

Follow the directions for shaping the pizzas on page 86. Place one piece of dough on the grill. Grill for about 1 minute, or until the underside of the dough is nicely browned. Using tongs, turn the dough over and grill for about 30 seconds longer, or until the underside of the dough is just stiffened. Remove to a baking sheet and repeat with the remaining dough rounds.

Brush the pizza crusts with the remaining 1 tablespoon basil oil. Arrange the eggplant and tomatoes on the crusts and sprinkle with the goat cheese. Grill the pizzas, 1 or 2 at a time, for 3 to 4 minutes, or until the cheese begins to soften. Sprinkle with the basil, drizzle with basil oil if desired, and serve.

> Grilled eggplant and goat cheese is a great combination. Top the pizza with a drizzle of basil oil (available at speciality food stores) and you have a wonderful vegetarian dish.

**1 medium-size eggplant (about 1 pound), cut into ¼-inch-thick slices**

**About 3 tablespoons basil oil**

**¾ teaspoon salt**

**¾ teaspoon freshly ground pepper**

**8 plum tomatoes, halved & seeded**

**1 recipe Pizza Dough (page 88), divided into 4 pieces**

**8 ounces fresh goat cheese, crumbled**

**¼ cup julienned fresh basil**

# TOMATO, MINT

**This is one of those quintes-sential summer dishes. When tomatoes are at their peak, I could probably eat this at every meal.**

*Serves 4*

PREHEAT THE GRILL to high and brush with oil.

Grill the tomato slices for about 1 minute on each side, just until charred. Remove from the grill.

Grill the bread for about 1 minute on each side, or until golden. Rub the cut sides of the garlic over the warm bread. Set aside.

Coarsely chop the tomatoes and put into a medium-size bowl along with the basil, mint, oil, salt, and pepper. Spoon the tomato mixture onto the bread, dividing it evenly. Serve immediately.

2 large firm tomatoes (about 1 pound), cut into ½-inch-thick slices

Four ½-inch-thick large slices country bread

1 garlic clove, halved

2 tablespoons chopped fresh basil

1 tablespoon chopped fresh mint

1 tablespoon extra-virgin olive oil

½ teaspoon kosher salt

½ teaspoon freshly ground pepper

**PEPPERS &**

*Serves 4*

**Italian Fontina is one of those versatile semi-soft cheeses that never lasts very long in my house. If you can't find it, you can substitute mozzarella.**

PREHEAT THE GRILL to high and brush with oil.

Grill the bell peppers, turning several times, for about 15 minutes, or until blackened on all sides. Transfer to a paper bag and let steam for 10 minutes. When cool enough to handle, peel, core, and seed the peppers. Coarsely chop them and put into a small bowl. Add 1 tablespoon of the oil, the garlic, oregano, salt, and red pepper flakes, tossing until mixed. Set aside.

Brush the bread with the remaining 1 tablespoon oil. Grill on one side for about 1 minute, or until golden. Remove and place the pepper mixture on the grilled side of the bread, dividing it evenly. Sprinkle the Fontina over the peppers and put the bread back on the grill for about 2 minutes, or until the cheese has melted and the underside of the bread is golden. Serve hot.

2 red bell peppers

2 tablespoons extra-virgin olive oil

1 garlic clove, mashed to a paste

½ teaspoon dried oregano, crumbled

½ teaspoon salt

⅛ teaspoon crushed red pepper flakes

Four ½-inch-thick large slices country bread

1 cup grated Italian Fontina cheese (4 ounces)

# MUSHROOM & PESTO

*Serves 4*

PREHEAT THE GRILL to high. Place a vegetable grill rack on top and brush with oil.

In a food processor, combine the basil, Parmesan, pignoli, garlic, ¼ teaspoon of the salt, and ¼ teaspoon of the pepper, and process to a coarse puree. With the machine running, add 2 tablespoons of the oil in a slow stream, processing until combined and thickened. Set aside.

In a small bowl, drizzle the remaining 2 tablespoons oil over the mushroom slices, sprinkle with the remaining ½ teaspoon each salt and pepper, and toss until evenly coated.

Grill the mushrooms for 2 to 3 minutes on each side, or until browned and tender. Grill the bread for about 1 minute on each side, or until golden.

Spread some of the pesto on the bread and top with the mushrooms. Serve hot, passing the remaining pesto on the side.

**This bruschetta would make any vegetarian (and plenty of nonvegetarians) happy at lunchtime. You can also toss the grilled mushrooms and pesto with some pasta for a terrific dinner.**

½ cup packed fresh
  basil leaves

2 tablespoons freshly grated
  Parmesan cheese

1 tablespoon pignoli
  (pine nuts)

1 small garlic clove, chopped

¾ teaspoon salt

¾ teaspoon freshly ground
  pepper

¼ cup extra-virgin olive oil

4 portobello mushrooms (4 to
  5 inches in diameter), stems
  removed, briefly rinsed &
  cut into ½-inch-thick slices

Four ½-inch-thick large slices
  country bread

# MOZZARELLA PANINI

**SAVORY**

**I have always loved anchovies, and in these panini (or small sandwiches) they play a rather prominent role. Mixed with chopped tomatoes, basil, and olive oil, they balance the mild flavor of the warm mozzarella.**

PREHEAT THE GRILL to medium-high and brush with oil.

With a large sharp knife, chop the anchovies and garlic together until a paste forms. Transfer to a small bowl and stir in the tomatoes, basil, oil, and pepper. Set aside.

Grill the bread on its cut side for about 1 minute, or until browned and crusty. Spread the tomato mixture on the bottom halves of the bread and top with the mozzarella. Put back onto the grill for about 2 minutes, or until the cheese begins to look soft and the underside of the bread is lightly browned. Top with the remaining bread and turn the panini over. Grill for about 1 minute longer, or until lightly browned on the bottom. Serve hot.

3 anchovy fillets

1 small garlic clove

2 plum tomatoes, finely chopped

3 tablespoons chopped fresh basil

1 tablespoon extra-virgin olive oil

½ teaspoon freshly ground pepper

1 large ciabatta bread, cut into 4 pieces & split, or other Italian loaf bread, cut into 4-inch lengths & split

8 ounces mozzarella cheese, thinly sliced

# SPINACH & RICOTTA

*Serves 4*

Some people might sniff at having to turn on their grill for this panini, and you can always use your broiler instead. Personally, I'd rather use a grill. The food tastes better, and it cooks faster.

PREHEAT THE GRILL to high and brush with oil.

Place the spinach, along with any water still clinging to the leaves, in a large skillet over high heat. Cook, stirring, for about 2 minutes, or until the spinach is wilted. Set aside until cool enough to handle. Using your hands, squeeze out as much water as possible. Coarsely chop the spinach and set aside.

In the same skillet, heat the oil over high heat until hot. Add the garlic and red pepper flakes and cook, stirring, for about 1 minute, or until the garlic is golden. Add the spinach, sprinkle with the salt, and cook, stirring constantly, for 1 to 2 minutes longer, or until the spinach is very hot. Remove from the heat and keep warm.

Grill the rolls for about 1 minute on each side, or until lightly browned. Divide the ricotta among the bottoms of the rolls and top with the spinach. Cover with the roll tops and serve.

2 bunches spinach (about 1½ pounds), stems trimmed & thoroughly washed

2 tablespoons extra-virgin olive oil

2 garlic cloves, chopped

¼ teaspoon crushed red pepper flakes

¼ teaspoon salt

4 crusty Italian sandwich rolls (about 4 inches in diameter), split in half

8 ounces ricotta salata cheese, thinly sliced

# ARUGULA PANINI

*Serves 4*

This is a truly luxurious sandwich. Fresh goat cheese is turned into an herbed spread for whole-grain country bread, which is then topped with grilled chicken and peppery arugula.

PREHEAT THE GRILL to high and brush with oil.

Brush the chicken with the oil and sprinkle with the salt and pepper. Grill the chicken for 3 to 4 minutes on each side, or until cooked through. Remove to a cutting board and let rest for 5 minutes.

Meanwhile, in a small bowl, combine the goat cheese, basil, parsley, garlic, and water, mixing with a fork until blended. Set aside.

Grill the bread for about 1 minute on each side, or until golden. Remove from the grill. Spread the goat cheese on the slices of bread. Using a sharp knife, slice the chicken across the grain, on the diagonal, into ¼-inch-thick slices and place on half of the bread. Top with the arugula and the remaining bread. Cut the panini in half on the diagonal and serve.

---

3 boneless skinless chicken breast halves (about 5 ounces each)

1 tablespoon extra-virgin olive oil

½ teaspoon salt

½ teaspoon freshly ground pepper

3 ounces fresh goat cheese, at room temperature

2 tablespoons chopped fresh basil

1 tablespoon chopped fresh flat-leaf parsley

1 small garlic clove, mashed to a paste

2 tablespoons cold water

8 thin slices whole-wheat country bread

1 bunch arugula, trimmed & washed

# DESSERTS

# GRILLED PEACHES

## RICOTTA WITH

**This dessert is unbelievably easy yet impressive to serve. No cooking is involved except for grilling the peaches. And the added bonus —it's very low in fat.**

IN A SMALL BOWL, combine the ricotta, 1 tablespoon of the brown sugar, the orange zest, and cinnamon, mixing well. Divide the ricotta among 4 oiled 6-ounce custard cups, pressing it down firmly into each cup. Cover and refrigerate for about 30 minutes.

Meanwhile, in a medium-size bowl, stir together the remaining 1 tablespoon brown sugar with the Amaretto. Add the peaches, tossing until coated. Set aside while the ricotta is chilling.

Preheat the grill to high. Set a vegetable grill rack on top and brush with oil.

Using a slotted spoon, remove the peaches from the bowl, reserving any accumulated juices. Grill the peaches for 2 to 3 minutes on each side, or until grill-marked and hot. Remove and set aside.

To unmold the ricotta cakes, run a small thin knife around the edge of the ricotta mixture to loosen it. Invert a custard cup over a serving plate and shake the cup up and down several times to release the ricotta, then remove the cup. Repeat with the remaining cups. Place the peaches around the ricotta cakes, drizzle with the reserved peach juice, and sprinkle with the amaretti crumbs. Serve immediately.

1 cup part-skim ricotta cheese

2 tablespoons packed brown sugar

1¼ teaspoons grated orange zest

⅛ teaspoon ground cinnamon

2 tablespoons Amaretto

1 pound ripe peaches (preferably freestone), halved, pitted & cut into ½-inch-thick wedges

6 amaretti cookies, crushed

# GRILLED FRUIT

*Serves 4*

**Make this compote with the season's best fruit and serve warm with vanilla gelato or frozen yogurt.**

PREHEAT THE GRILL to high. Put a vegetable grill rack on top and brush with oil.

In a medium-size bowl, stir the rum and brown sugar together until blended. Add the plums, peaches, figs, and pear slices, tossing until coated. Set aside for 15 minutes.

Using a slotted spoon, remove the fruit from the bowl, reserving the accumulated juices. Grill the fruit, turning once, for 2 to 3 minutes on each side, or until grill-marked and hot. Remove to a serving bowl. Pour the reserved juices over, add the berries, and toss gently to mix. Let stand at room temperature for about 30 minutes.

3 tablespoons dark rum

2 tablespoons packed brown sugar

6 Italian prune plums (about 8 ounces), halved & pitted

3 small peaches or nectarines (preferably freestone), halved, pitted & cut into ½-inch-thick wedges

4 small ripe figs, halved

1 large ripe pear, peeled, cored & cut into ½-inch-thick wedges

1 cup blackberries, blueberries, or raspberries

# GRILLED PEAR & ORANGE SALAD

*Serves 4*

Here's a simple grilled dessert that looks very pretty on a rustic round platter. To keep the pear slices looking neat, use a melon baller to remove the cores.

PREHEAT THE GRILL to medium-high and brush with oil.

In a medium-size bowl, toss the pear and orange slices with the sugar, lemon zest, and lemon juice. Let stand 5 minutes.

Using a slotted spoon, remove the fruit from the bowl, reserving the juices. Grill the pears and oranges for 2 to 5 minutes on each side, or until nicely marked and bubbling. Arrange the orange slices around the outside of a large round platter and place the pear slices in the center. Stir the liqueur into the reserved fruit juices and drizzle over the fruit. Let stand at room temperature for 30 minutes, or serve slightly chilled.

3 firm Bosc or D'Anjou pears (about 1½ pounds), peeled, cored & cut into ½-inch-thick wedges

3 navel oranges, washed & cut into ¼-inch-thick slices

¼ cup sugar

2 teaspoons grated lemon zest

2 tablespoons fresh lemon juice

1 tablespoon orange liqueur

# RICOTTA BRUSCHETTA

*Serves 4*

**Since I am a bread addict, this is my idea of a great dessert. Actually, it makes a terrific breakfast as well.**

PREHEAT THE GRILL to high and brush with oil.

Combine the ricotta, 1 tablespoon of the honey, and the thyme in a small bowl, mixing well. Set aside.

In a medium-size bowl, combine the remaining 2 tablespoons honey and the raspberry liqueur, stirring until blended. Add the berries and gently toss until coated. Set aside.

Lightly brush the bread with the melted butter.

Grill the bread, turning once, for 1 to 2 minutes on each side, or until grill-marked and hot. Remove to serving plates and spread with the ricotta mixture. Spoon the berries on top and serve.

1 cup part-skim ricotta cheese

3 tablespoons honey

2 teaspoons chopped fresh thyme

1 tablespoon raspberry liqueur

1½ cups mixed berries such as blackberries, raspberries, and/or blueberries

Four ½-inch-thick large slices country bread

1 tablespoon unsalted butter, melted

# PANETTONE WITH

R

*Serves 4*

PREHEAT THE GRILL to high and brush with oil.

In a small saucepan, combine the apricots, orange juice, and sugar over high heat. Bring to a boil and cook, stirring occasionally, for 2 minutes, or until the juice has reduced to ½ cup. Remove from the heat and stir in the raspberries and liqueur. Set aside.

Lightly brush the panettone on both sides with the butter. Grill for 2 to 3 minutes on each side, or until grill-marked and hot. Transfer to serving plates, spoon the fruit with its juices on top, and serve.

**Since panettone and similar cakes are available only at Christmas and Easter, substitute pound cake or brioche when necessary. To cut the apricots, use kitchen scissors lightly sprayed with vegetable oil cooking spray.**

⅓ cup dried apricots, snipped into small pieces

¾ cup fresh orange juice

1 tablespoon sugar

2 half-pints fresh raspberries or 1½ cups frozen, thawed

1 tablespoon orange liqueur

Four 1-inch-thick slices panettone, brioche, or pound cake

2 tablespoons unsalted butter, melted

RASPBERRIES

**This sweet polenta is a some-what low-fat dessert, so a bit of whipped cream or vanilla gelato would not harm it a bit.**

*Serves 4 to 6*

IN A MEDIUM-SIZE HEAVY-bottomed saucepan, heat the milk, water, sugar, raisins, and salt over high heat, stirring frequently, until bubbles form around the edges. Whisking constantly in one direction, slowly add the polenta in a thin stream. Reduce the heat to medium-low and cook, stirring constantly with a wooden spoon, for 2 to 4 minutes, or until the polenta is very thick and creamy and begins to pull away from the sides of the pan. Remove from the heat and stir in the vanilla.

Pour the polenta onto a baking sheet. Using a narrow spatula, spread it into a 10-x 7-inch rectangle. Set aside until firm.

Preheat the grill to high and brush generously with oil.

Cut the polenta into 8 triangles. Brush the polenta and nectarines with the melted butter. Grill the polenta and nectarines for 2 to 3 minutes on each side, or until nicely marked and hot. Transfer the polenta to serving plates. Cut the nectarines into thick wedges and place on top of the polenta. Sprinkle with the chocolate and almonds and serve.

2½ cups whole or low-fat (2%) milk

1 cup water

¼ cup plus 2 tablespoons sugar

¼ cup golden raisins

¼ teaspoon salt

1 cup imported instant polenta (about 6 ounces)

1 teaspoon vanilla extract

4 large nectarines, preferably freestone (about 2 pounds), pitted & quartered

2 tablespoons unsalted butter, melted

2 tablespoons grated bitter-sweet chocolate

1 tablespoon plus 1 teaspoon sliced almonds, toasted

*Serves 8*

My friends Barbara and David are amazing gardeners who cultivate endless varieties of vegetables, fruits, and flowers. The first time I met them was at the end of August, and their Italian plum tree was bursting with fruit. Here's the tart I created to help clean up their lawn.

PREHEAT THE OVEN to 350°F.

Prepare the crust: In a food processor, combine the amaretti, breadcrumbs, and pignoli. Process, pulsing, until finely ground. Add the butter and process until the mixture is evenly moistened. Press the crumb mixture onto the bottom of a 9-inch tart pan with a removable bottom. Bake for 8 to 10 minutes, or until the crust is lightly toasted. Set aside.

Prepare the filling: In a food processor, combine the ricotta, eggs, egg white, sugar, vanilla, and salt. Process until smooth. Pour into the baked crust, spreading it evenly with a rubber spatula. Bake for 25 to 30 minutes, or just until set. Set aside and let cool.

Preheat the grill to high and brush with oil.

Grill the plums on their cut side for 1 to 2 minutes, or until lightly browned and beginning to bubble. Remove and cut into ½-inch-thick wedges. Arrange the plum slices in concentric circles on top of the tart filling.

In a small saucepan, melt the jelly over medium-low heat. Brush the jelly over the plums. Let the tart stand until the jelly sets.

To serve, remove the pan sides and place the tart on a serving plate. Serve at room temperature or slightly chilled.

### CRUST

- 1½ cups amaretti cookies (about 3 ounces)
- ½ cup dried breadcrumbs
- ⅓ cup pignoli (pine nuts)
- ¼ cup (½ stick) unsalted butter, melted

### FILLING

- One 15½-ounce container part-skim ricotta cheese
- 2 large eggs
- 1 large egg white
- ⅓ cup sugar
- 1 teaspoon vanilla extract
- ¼ teaspoon salt

- 1½ pounds Italian prune plums, halved & pitted
- ¼ cup red currant jelly

# INDEX

# CONVERSION TABLE

## LENGTH

| U.S. Measurements | Metrics |
|---|---|
| $\frac{1}{8}$ inch | 3 mm |
| $\frac{1}{4}$ inch | 6 mm |
| $\frac{3}{8}$ inch | 1 cm |
| $\frac{1}{2}$ inch | 1.2 cm |
| $\frac{3}{4}$ inch | 2 cm |
| 1 inch | 2.5 cm |
| $1\frac{1}{4}$ inches | 3.1 cm |
| $1\frac{1}{2}$ inches | 3.7 cm |
| 2 inches | 5 cm |
| 3 inches | 7.5 cm |
| 4 inches | 10 cm |
| 5 inches | 12.5 cm |

## WEIGHTS

| Ounces and Pounds | Metrics |
|---|---|
| $\frac{1}{4}$ ounce | 7 grams |
| $\frac{1}{3}$ ounce | 10 g |
| $\frac{1}{2}$ ounce | 14 g |
| 1 ounce | 28 g |
| $1\frac{1}{2}$ ounces | 42 g |
| $1\frac{3}{4}$ ounces | 50 g |
| 2 ounces | 57 g |
| 3 ounces | 85 g |
| $3\frac{1}{2}$ ounces | 100 g |
| 4 ounces ($\frac{1}{4}$ pound) | 114 g |
| 6 ounces | 170 g |
| 8 ounces ($\frac{1}{2}$ pound) | 227 g |
| 9 ounces | 250 g |
| 16 ounces (1 pound) | 464 g |

## LIQUID MEASURES

tsp.: teaspoon/Tbs.: tablespoon

| Spoons and Cups | | Metric Equivalents |
|---|---|---|
| $\frac{1}{4}$ | tsp. | 1.23 milliliters |
| $\frac{1}{2}$ | tsp. | 2.5 ml |
| $\frac{3}{4}$ | tsp. | 3.7 ml |
| 1 | tsp. | 5 ml |
| 1 | dessertspoon | 10 ml |
| 1 | Tbs. (3 tsp.) | 15 ml |
| 2 | Tbs. (1 ounce) | 30 ml |
| $\frac{1}{4}$ | cup | 60 ml |
| $\frac{1}{3}$ | cup | 80 ml |
| $\frac{1}{2}$ | cup | 120 ml |
| $\frac{2}{3}$ | cup | 160 ml |
| $\frac{3}{4}$ | cup | 180 ml |
| 1 | cup (8 ounces) | 240 ml |
| 2 | cups (1 pint) | 480 ml |
| 3 | cups | 720 ml |
| 4 | cups (1 quart) | 1 liter |
| 4 | quarts (1 gallon) | 3.75 liters |

## TEMPERATURE

| °F (Fahrenheit) | | °C (Centigrade or Celsius) |
|---|---|---|
| 32 | (water freezes) | 0 |
| 200 | | 95 |
| 212 | (water boils) | 100 |
| 250 | | 120 |
| 275 | | 135 |
| 300 | (slow oven) | 150 |
| 325 | | 160 |
| 350 | (moderate oven) | 175 |
| 375 | | 190 |
| 400 | (hot oven) | 205 |
| 425 | | 220 |
| 450 | (very hot oven) | 232 |
| 475 | | 245 |
| 500 | (extremely hot oven) | 260 |

## APPROXIMATE EQUIVALENTS

1 kilo is slightly more than 2 pounds
1 liter is slightly more than 1 quart
1 meter is slightly over 3 feet
1 centimeter is approximately $\frac{3}{8}$ inch